ADVERTISING FOR BOOKS

DALE L. ROBERTS

Advertising for Books: A Guide to Promoting & Selling with the Largest Online Bookseller

Copyright ©2024 by One Jacked Monkey LLC
All rights reserved.

No portion of this book may be reproduced in any form without written permission from the publisher or author, except as permitted by U.S. copyright law.

eBook ISBN: 978-1-63925-041-7
Paperback ISBN: 978-1-63925-042-4
Hardcover ISBN: 978-1-63925-043-1
Audiobook ISBN: 978-1-63925-044-8

All rights reserved. No part of this book may be reproduced in any form by any electronic or mechanical means, including information storage and retrieval systems, without permission in writing from the copyright owner, except by a reviewer who may quote brief passages in a review.

Some recommended links in this book are part of affiliate programs. This means if you purchase a product through one of the links, then I get a portion of each sale. It doesn't affect your cost and helps support the cause. If you have any reservations about buying a product through my affiliate link, then Google a direct link and bypass the affiliate link.

CONTENTS

INTRODUCTION 1

EXPECTATIONS VS. REALITY: WHY ARE AMAZON ADS SO DIFFICULT? 6

WHAT IS RELEVANCE? 19

KNOWING THE TERMINOLOGY 26

WHAT ADS FUNCTION BEST FOR BOOKS? 37

HOW TO SET UP & MANAGE AN AMAZON AD 47

ANALYZING THE DATA TO OPTIMIZE THE AD 86

TROUBLESHOOTING A PROBLEMATIC AD 105

CONCLUSION 112

A SMALL ASK... 115

ABOUT THE AUTHOR 118

SPECIAL THANKS 119

RESOURCES 120

REFERENCES 121

GET MY BESTSELLER BOOK LAUNCH CHECKLIST ABSOLUTELY FREE!

Want to launch your book to bestseller status on Amazon? Sign up for my email newsletter today and get my **Bestseller Book Launch Checklist** for FREE! This step-by-step plan will help you make your book a hit.

But that's not all! When you subscribe, you'll also get my email newsletter packed with the latest self-publishing news and tips. Get all you need to know in just one or two emails per week.

Subscribe now and grab your free checklist at
DaleLinks.com/Checklist

Next level tools to help you grow.

Whether you're an aspiring author or international bestseller, we've got the tools to help you publish faster, distribute wider and manage your business easier.

Learn more by going to **d2d.tips/dale** and read on to discover some of what sets D2D apart:

- ✓ Automated end-matter
- ✓ New Release Notifications for readers
- ✓ Payment Splitting for contributors
- ✓ Scheduled price changes
- ✓ Smashwords store coupons
- ✓ Universal Book Links via Books2Read.com

 **It's print-on-demand reimagined.**

Create a paperback on draft2digital.com from your existing ebook with just a few clicks, and **create a full, wrap-around book cover from your ebook cover**. It really is that easy!

Massive annual sales, self-serve promotion tools, and the **industry's best royalty rates** of up to 80% list. Readers love discovering breakout indie authors at smashwords.com.

Win **awards** and get **reviews** for **your book**

25% off your first purchase

bookawardpro.com

"I've used dozens of book cover design services over the last ten years, and none compare to the level of quality and professionalism that Miblart delivers."

— *Dale L. Roberts*

Miblart - a book cover design company for self-published authors

Designers who specialize in different genres	Unlimited number of revisions
No deposit to get started	You can pay in installments

GET A BOOK COVER THAT WILL BECOME YOUR N°1 MARKETING TOOL

Excellent

★★★★★ 4.9

Your Best Friend for Book Advertising

Meet **Dibbly Create.**

Your All-in-1 A.I. companion for writing, publishing & marketing your book.

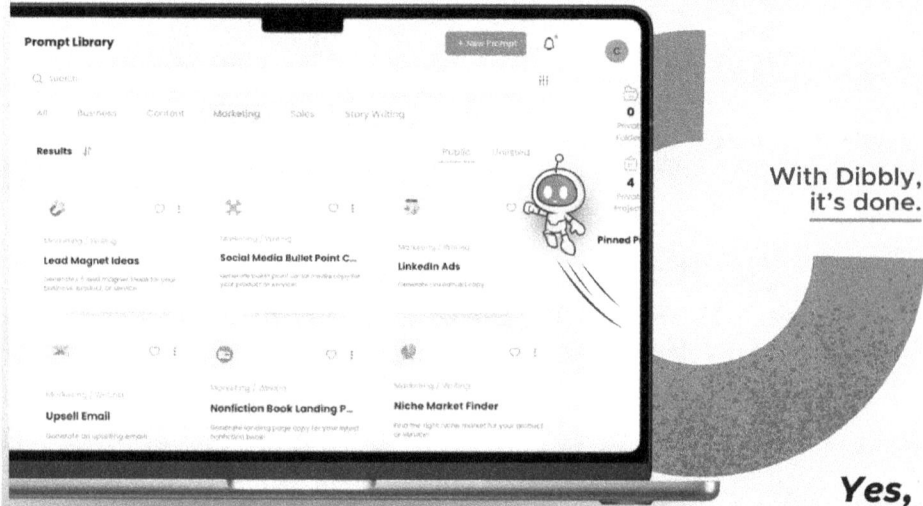

With Dibbly, it's done.

A.I. Assisted:

- ✓ Book descriptions
- ✓ Lead magnet
- ✓ Email copy
- ✓ Subject lines
- ✓ Social media posts
- ✓ Press releases
- ✓ Landing pages
- ✓ Much more

Yes,
I Need Help Marketing my Book

Try for Free!

Scan the QR Code or visit dibbly.com/create

INTRODUCTION

I was broke, angry, and beyond frustrated. For a couple of years, I bought into somebody else's dream, even at the expense of my bank account and my marriage. Sure, this is all on me. I own every bit of it. However, it doesn't stop me from feeling a sense of regret or reflecting on time wasted working in a multi-level marketing company (MLM).

They sold my wife and me on the dream of quitting our nine-to-five jobs and being our own bosses. All it took was investing in the MLM supplement company for a hefty sum of $1,200. Oh, and that's not all. If I invested more and recruited more people to hawk more goods, then I'd win big. Let's not forget how we had to attend every local meeting and mixer, bring a friend with us, and put on happy faces despite deeply sinking into the red for our so-called business.

This MLM company had great products that I was happy to take myself. However, they built a culture around doing what they said and not questioning them one bit. While our bank account drained to support the cause, our friendships dwindled. Before long, it was just my wife and me against the world. I felt like that was all I needed—to be backed into a corner and come out fighting.

Boy, was I wrong! We lost a ton of time and resources because someone, more specifically a company, had sold us a bill of goods. Finally, we had to decide: do we keep going down this path or quit while we're ahead?

With a heavy heart, I called my mentor in the MLM business and explained our situation. Little did I know that he'd curse me out and leave me feeling worse for opening myself up to him in the first place. He was downright ugly and made sure I felt his anger.

After hanging up the phone, I felt an overwhelming sense of relief. I no longer had to feel weird and do creepy sales tactics to put food on my table. I didn't have to buy into some company's mission statement and overall brand goals. My wife and I could officially work against the world on our terms.

Skip forward a few years after that day. We broke away from the MLM company and the two of us successfully started running our own work-from-home businesses. We didn't have to invest any more than we wanted to put into it. In fact, I truly believe when I cut ties with that company, I wholeheartedly devoted my time to the business of self-publishing. The rest is history.

What exactly does a story about an MLM company have to do with Amazon Advertising? Well, I'm not comparing Amazon Ads to a sketchy direct marketing company, but to the way we go into it. If you go into advertising books on Amazon with the mindset of throwing money at problems, then you're definitely going to lose big time.

Amazon Advertising is one of the best ways to promote your book today. The system is simple, yet nearly impossible to master. While

INTRODUCTION

some would-be gurus and overnight experts would have you believe Amazon Ads can be easy, the reality is it's even easier to waste a ton of money without getting anything in return.

I don't want you go down that dusty road and waste all your money and time on some get-rich-quick scheme. No, you will not get a ticket to my local mixer where I boast about making millions with Amazon Ads. You won't have to worry about me disowning you if things don't turn out the way you like. The fact is Amazon Ads aren't for everyone.

However, I'm confident by the time you're done with this book, you'll have a better understanding of how to start, launch, and monitor ad campaigns. Then, you can decide if running Amazon Ads is for you. Keep in mind that results may vary, and I'm not saying you *have* to spend money on Amazon Ads to sell books.

Amazon Advertising is merely a tool in your box of marketing and promotional strategies. Much like an unused socket wrench set, you can leave it alone until you're ready to use it. When the time comes and you're financially able to invest in Amazon Ads, then you can bring it out of your toolbox and put it to good use.

Just remember this one fact:

Do not invest what you cannot stand to lose.

Yep, I'm literally telling you it's possible to invest thousands and lose it all. I'm not trying to scare you away from running ads on Amazon; I'm just sharing the reality. Though I can offer every strategy and tip in my arsenal, I can't assure you'll have massive success. However, I'm confident if you ease your way into using Amazon

Advertising for books, you'll mitigate any financial loss and increase your understanding of ads.

Judging by the fact you picked up this book, you probably:

1. Are an author
2. Are looking to run Amazon Ads for your books
3. Want to improve your understanding of Amazon Ads

If you fit one of these roles, then you've come to the right place. I'm going to get granular with Amazon Advertising. I'll lean heavily on my experience spending thousands on countless campaigns, earning multiple certifications in Amazon Advertising, and gleaning insights from other successful self-published authors who have used ads to bolster sales.

I have good news for you!

First, you don't have to worry about investing anything in Amazon Ads. Simply focus on getting through this book first, then circle back around when you launch your campaigns. Next, you won't have to spend anything beyond what you've invested in this book right now. Last, if you get to the end of this book still feeling like Amazon Ads may not be for you, at least you didn't invest thousands of dollars to find out.

Now, if you're one of these types of people who:

- Believe I'll provide the secret to success
- Want to get rich quick overnight
- Don't want to put in the work
- Don't have the money to invest in ads

INTRODUCTION

… then I won't have what you need. Simply close this book since you'll be better off without it. I will not pump you up or give you a bunch of hot trash. Anyone who tells you that self-publishing is easy money has an agenda or ulterior motive. Also, if anyone tells you ads only work for specific genres or popular authors, they're wrong.

Amazon Advertising can and will work for almost anybody, but it takes time, testing, flexibility, and good old-fashioned hard work. If you're ready, willing, and able to do that, then let's dig in!

EXPECTATIONS VS. REALITY: WHY ARE AMAZON ADS SO DIFFICULT?

I've repeatedly heard from aspiring authors and established self-publishers that Amazon Advertising is hard, too expensive, or not suited to certain niches. While learning Amazon Advertising isn't easy, the process can be rather simple if you give it time, attention, and some flexibility.

Can it be expensive? Sure, if you let it.

You're in good hands though because I *hate* losing money or spending it frivolously on marketing. Do not invest thousands of dollars into advertising until you have a firm grasp on advertising basics. You first need to know the process, what brings you results, and how you can optimize your ads to pull in more book sales.

As for the myth that Amazon Advertising is only good for specific niches, that's 100% wrong. Quite a few fiction and nonfiction authors—and even low-content book publishers—use Amazon Advertising to great success. Why is that? Because they don't simply settle on pumping a bunch of money into the Amazon Ads machine hoping it'll spit back money like a broken ATM. Every time someone comes to me for advice on Amazon Advertising, inevitably, they say it didn't work, the niche is saturated, the keywords are too competitive to bid for, and so on. The reality is they just didn't know what they were doing.

Sometimes, authors just threw money at Amazon Ads and hoped for the best. While other times, authors watched a few videos on my channel, took a course hosted by a famous author, or simply got advice from some random Facebook Group mastermind. While those methods alone aren't bad, combined, the author absolutely must separate fact from fiction. Not to mention, they still have to make sense of what they curated, decipher it, and make the most of what they have left over.

The next *biggest* problem is most authors are blind to whether their book is packaged effectively. While you might think your book cover is on the money, the book description is perfect, and you priced your book competitively in your niche, the reality is if you aren't getting sales *without* ads, then something is fundamentally wrong with your book.

The fundamentals to any good-selling book include:

- Great book cover
- Killer book description
- Competitive price point

Having invested hours in your book, I can only imagine you think highly of it. Why wouldn't you? You poured your heart into every page, so you should be rather fond of your publication. Sadly, it's that bias that can get you into hot water and leave you in no-man's-land where readers will never find you. Even when a potential reader finds your title, if you don't have any of those three fundamentals dialed in, then all is lost.

Sure, you can have an ugly cover and still sell copies if your book description does a great job of closing the sale. Or you could have a stellar cover, but your book description isn't convincing anyone to buy it. Of course, if you bargain-basement price your book, then many people might view it as cheap or inferior. But if you price your book far above others in your niche, you run the risk of readers thinking you're overvaluing your content.

Why am I so focused on the fundamentals of book publishing rather than Amazon Advertising? If you can't dial in the fundamentals, how can you ever expect to get results from ads? Yes, even a blind squirrel can get a nut, but why put the cart before the horse?

While having a bad book cover, poor marketing description, and questionable pricing might not stop you from using Amazon Ads, your conversion rate isn't going to be high. Instead of aiming for a realistic and attainable closing rate per click, your ratio could be closer to one out of every one hundred clicks. The more clicks you have on an ad, the more you pay and the less you make—unless that click converts to a sale. But one sale per hundred clicks is not a formula for running a profitable ad campaign. Ideally, a decent conversion ratio would be one sale out of every ten to twenty clicks, so long as all the previous elements are on point.

You want to have those three fundamental elements showroom ready, so when you spend money to send traffic to your book's page, people are more prepared, receptive, and happy to buy your book. Here's how this scenario could play out:

EXPECTATIONS VS. REALITY: WHY ARE AMAZON ADS SO DIFFICULT?

1. The browsing customer searches for their interests on Amazon.
2. Sixteen products are returned on the first page of search results, plus ads interspersed through those organic results.
3. The browsing customer sees your ad and has a decision to make, whether conscious or subconscious. Does the book cover look like something they'd enjoy? If yes, they may click on the ad to go to the product page. If not, they'll scroll past the ad, never giving your book a second thought. The good news is if the customer never clicks on your ad, then you aren't charged for that customer seeing it, so you won't lose any money.
4. After the customer clicks on the ad, they have another decision to make. Will they buy immediately based on the cover? Possibly, but that doesn't happen too often, especially if you don't have an established following. The customer usually does one of two things: reads the book description or reads the reviews. Once the consumer has the information, they need to decide whether or not to buy the book, they will either purchase yours or return to the search results.
5. Now, comes the tricky part. Let's assume the customer decides to give your book a chance. That person won't finally click that buy button if the pricing doesn't align with what's conveyed in the book description or on the cover. It's mission critical to get your pricing set at a rate that makes sense and is in alignment with the value proposition.

Since I'm trying to demonstrate the value of getting the essentials right, let's tackle the tough question: how do you know if your fundamentals are good? If you're getting consistent sales daily, you're probably on the right track. However, if you're not seeing consistent results, then you'll need to make some tweaks before you invest in ads. Here are a few tips to get those elements right.

Before you ever settle on a book cover, study the Amazon marketplace in your niche and note all the books at the top of the charts. What are the common themes, layouts, and color schemes? How can you best embody those elements? I'm not suggesting you directly lift someone's intellectual property. And I won't have the answers for you in this book. You'll have to lean on your intuition and research for this step. Once you find the right elements, then hire a professional cover designer or do it yourself.

The next step is going to be a simple one, and I encourage you to use this method every year. Get a thumbnail mockup of your ebook cover and take a screenshot of the bestseller list for your niche. Place your book at the number one spot, just over the current #1 bestseller. Now, look at the competitors in your niche. Does your cover fit in with the rest? Does it stand out in a good way or a bad way?

If it's the latter option, then go back to the drawing board. If your cover stands out in a good way, test it out. Share your screenshot with several peers in the industry; you get bonus points for having someone within your niche evaluate it. Be ready to take it on the chin because your peers should tell you the reality. Your baby might be ugly, but thankfully it's not permanent. Adjust and go through this step again.

Join my Discord community to connect and network with other authors. With nearly 1,000 active members, you'll find a few great people to offer assistance with your cover.

DaleLinks.com/Discord

Should you find book sales dipping a bit, then go back through this vetting process again. While the cover might have worked a year ago, that doesn't mean it'll work now. Be open enough to accept that if your cover doesn't convert as well as it used to, then it's time to switch it out for an updated design. Is this going to be costly and time-consuming? Yes, but it can be worth it, especially if your sales are suffering.

The book description can be a bit more problematic. Authors are great at writing their books, but when it's time to describe that book in a way that compels readers to buy, they're often at a loss.

Hey, don't sweat it! I totally get it. That's why I lean heavily on copywriters to create book descriptions for me. Copywriting is the ability to write content that entices prospective customers to buy. It's not sleazy and is 100% ethical, as long as you deliver on the value proposition within the ad copy.

If you're not running ads, it can be tough to know whether the book cover, book description, or pricing are to blame for a lack of sales. Using Amazon Advertising, you can infer that the lack of sales comes from poor ad copy. For example, if someone clicks on your ad, we can assume the topic and cover matches the potential buyer's interests. If they do not buy your book after clicking the ad, then you can assume the buyer's resistance is caused by one of two things: bad ad copy or poor pricing.

Prolific author and book description expert Brian Meeks has shared how the price point can be what you want, so long as the ad copy is enticing enough to merit a higher premium. You can price your book high, and possibly higher than most in your niche, but you *must* have the ad copy to back it up.

This leads me to the last fundamental element—pricing. Quite a few authors don't know how to price their book, and they fearfully cling to ridiculously low prices in hopes they won't scare away customers. While some readers specifically look for cheap books, a vast majority of readers are simply looking for a solution to their problems. If that pain point is high enough for that potential reader, then no amount of money will be a roadblock. There are exceptions to that rule, of course. But in most instances, when a reader *really* wants what they're looking for and you validate that search, then they're most likely going to buy the product.

ASSUMING THE FUNDAMENTALS ARE PERFECT

Now, comes the fun stuff, right? Well, not so fast. There's more to running ads on Amazon than you know. Let's just assume your book has the perfect cover, ad copy, and pricing. Now you're ready to run ads, right? Sure, but you must temper your expectations with reality. Simply having those fundamentals alone doesn't ensure success with ads. You merely increase your odds of winning at advertising.

In the Amazon Advertising Certification course[i], Amazon teaches that advertisers need to get their products retail-ready before investing in ads. Why is this?

EXPECTATIONS VS. REALITY: WHY ARE AMAZON ADS SO DIFFICULT?

As much as Amazon likes your money, they also like their customer's money. If you win at ads, then they win at ads two-fold. You pay them for the ad placement and customers buy the product.

Specifically, Amazon states that for your product to be retail-ready, you must have:

1. **Clear and accurate product images.** Remember how we discussed the importance of a killer book cover? Well, this further validates what I shared previously. Don't be confused by this. The only product images you'll provide are through your KDP dashboard or through the publishing platform you use (i.e., IngramSpark, Lulu, etc.). Outside of opening an Amazon Seller Account (which costs a monthly premium to use), you won't be able to add images beyond your cover. You still have valuable real estate elsewhere on the product page, so don't sweat this too much.

2. **Accurate and descriptive product titles.** Again, Amazon wants you to convert browsing customers into buyers. Having your title, subtitle, series name, author name, and description error-free are of the utmost importance. Sure, you can skip hiring out a copywriter and can even get away with a boring description. What Amazon doesn't want is book metadata with improper placement or misleading text.

3. **Over an average 3.5-star rating.** Getting reviews on a new book can be problematic. It feels like the chicken or the egg situation. What comes first: getting the reviews or launching the book? How do you get reviews if the book isn't available yet? Rather than waste time telling you how to do it, I

highly recommend you check out my book *Amazon Reviews for Books* to find out exactly how to get reviews before and after your book launch.

4. **Over fifteen reviews.** In fact, Amazon stated in their ad certification course that 91% of browsing customers look at the reviews before they buy a product. That's pretty wild information that I wish I had years ago. Everyone just assumes getting more reviews is a good thing, but the theories and speculative number of reviews varies from fifty to one hundred to get meaningful results. To set the record straight, that number is not fifty, it's fifteen. That's not to say that fifty won't be effective when running ads, but at least you know the bare minimum you should have before you run ads.

5. **Enhanced content.** Slowly but surely, Amazon rolled out enhanced content for authors. Enhanced content features include the editorial review section and the From the Publisher section (aka A+ Content). To access the editorial review section, visit Author Central at Author.Amazon.com to set up your author profile.

6. **From the Publisher** is available through the Kindle Direct Publishing dashboard in the A+ Content section of the Marketing tab. You can post images, graphs, charts, and more. The nice part? A+ Content is fully indexable. When you post A+ Content to your product page, you further optimize your book for discoverability.

7. **Available inventory.** Since you're running a self-publishing business through Kindle Direct Publishing, you shouldn't

have an issue with inventory not being available. After all, it will be printed on demand, right? For ebooks and downloadable audiobooks, you should never have an Out of Stock tag on your product page. Print products can be a little more problematic if you publish to Amazon through aggregate publishers like IngramSpark, Draft2Digital, Lulu, or Blurb.

For reasons unknown, Amazon puts an Out of Stock tag on third-party print on demand companies. Many insiders and experts have speculated why, but no one has a definitive answer. To avoid any heartache or issues, run ads to products you fulfill through KDP. If all you have is the ebook published through KDP and the print book fulfilled through another company, then send traffic through your ebook. Once a customer lands on your product page, they'll have choices, and if your print book is out of stock, at least they can buy the ebook or audiobook.

Now that we know Amazon's thought process with advertising on their platform, what can we expect from their ads? Can we simply use their checklist, dump a bunch of money into ads, and expect big results?

Again, you increase your odds of success with all the items I've discussed in place, but that doesn't assure you of a clear victory right away. In fact, you might find your first ad does absolutely nothing when it launches. That's okay, because Amazon Advertising is a complex beast, and you have many things to consider before making the jump into ads.

Realistically, you can expect ads to have a certain life span, especially if you aren't monitoring and adjusting your ad campaigns daily. Is there a shelf life or expiration of an ad?

Yes and no.

Do you recall how we covered the importance of a killer book cover and how you may have to change it now and then? The same holds true for ads. While an ad might perform well for an extended period, it might just altogether stop delivering. Why is that?

Relevance—a topic we'll be covering in depth soon in this book.

Ultimately, Amazon has an algorithm that decides what works best for each customer based on their previous shopping and browsing history, as well as similar customer buying experiences. When Amazon serves an ad, they want that ad to convert browsing customers into buyers. If that ad can't prove itself, then Amazon will stop using it or require you to invest an exorbitant amount into the ad to keep it serving.

While it's commendable for you to try and make an ad work at a higher budget, I wouldn't recommend it. Even if you increase your daily budget and cost per click, you can't expect an underperforming ad to convert. That's one of the biggest issues with authors advertising books—throwing money at the problem. Now, if you're okay with pumping money into one book because you have a deep backend for sales or a series of books, then go ahead. Be forewarned though, driving non-buyers to your book isn't a good idea, even at a higher amount.

Once you get an ad that performs well and consistently, then chances are likely the relevance of that ad increases, and Amazon will be more apt to serve it to more customers. You won't have to do anything other than let it ride, scrape the data, adjust bids, and add targeting to make the ad perform better. It's kind of nice when you catch lightning in a bottle the first time and it will make you even more interested in seeing your ads succeed. Enjoy the feeling while it lasts, because even the best ads will peter out and dry up. Before that happens, you should have enough data to start a new ad, so as the old ad dies, you can create a new one that replaces it.

Robert G. Ryan shared his thoughts about ad lifespan in his book *Amazon Ads Unleashed*. With his extensive experience in Google Ads, he saw a correlation between Google Ads and Amazon Ads. He shared how an ad will die if it isn't run effectively and optimized over time. I had ads that ran for over two years with decent results, so this measures up. If your ads are dying, you'll need to take a deeper look at why.

Sometimes, an ad can fail because your targeting is slightly off. While you might target a keyword that *seems* to fit your book, it might not convert so well. For every impression, click, or buy missed on an ad, your ad's relevance drops for the targeted keyword. Having a poor-performing targeted keyword can bring down the relevancy of your ad; therefore, Amazon is less apt to serve it.

We're getting deep into the weeds and bringing out some terminology and theories you don't know just yet. Just stick with me, and you'll get a better idea of what all of this means.

Ads take time, practice, and testing. Sure, it won't be easy at first, but in due time, if you apply yourself, you'll see results. In the meantime, adjust your expectations with the reality of advertising on Amazon. It's difficult and certainly not for everyone. Take your time, apply the fundamentals from this book, and experiment with some strategies I'll share later, and I'm confident you'll be off to a better start with Amazon Advertising. Just remember that no one can guarantee results, so do lots of research (including this book) before investing any money.

WHAT IS RELEVANCE?

If you've been in the online business industry for long enough, you'll hear the word "relevance" tossed around quite a bit. What exactly does relevancy mean? How does it affect book sales? It's a rather deep topic, hence why I devoted an entire chapter to discussing the importance of relevancy in your book sales and ad campaigns.

We can view relevancy in two ways: perceived relevance and algorithmic relevance. When we determine, through experience and intuition, the relevance of an item online based on the niche, then that's perceived relevance. Often, people believe they can trust their intuition to guide them to the right outcome for relevance. Sure, your perception can help determine the best relevance for a title, but it doesn't mean it holds weight online. That's where algorithmic relevance comes into play.

Almost every facet of online business relies on a search engine. When a customer searches for a specific term or product, the search engine gets to work delivering the results best suited to that person. Quite a few factors contribute to building relevancy and not every customer will have the same search results. Why is that? Because an algorithm, a complex mathematical formula, determines what works best for each individual and their search. A few of those factors include:

1. Previous search history
2. Previous engagement (i.e., purchases on Amazon)
3. Other similar actions from similar audiences

To put this into simple terms, let's look at a somewhat real-world situation.

You arrive at a party where many people are hanging out. Small and large clusters of people are gathered together. When you approach one conversation, you notice the topic doesn't interest you, so you move on. At that moment, you don't perceive the relevance of the topic to your interests. As you move from circle to circle, you find many conversations fun yet not quite to your taste. Eventually, you land in a small circle of people chatting about arm wrestling championships—that's your jam! The conversation is popping, and everyone is having a good time talking about all things arm wrestling. You finally found a topic you perceive as relevant to your interests.

Now, imagine you go into a party, but instead of going from one conversation to the next trying to find your interests, you have a robot figure it out for you in a split second. The robot knows what everyone is talking about, who is moving between one conversation and another, people who were previously involved in the conversation, and where they went. Then, the robot plugs in all the data into a complex mathematical formula to get the results best suited to your needs. You come in and tell the robot you love to chat about arm wrestling. It immediately whisks you away to the conversation best suited to your satisfaction. Will it get it right every time? No, but the more this robot gets to know your interests, habits, and other information, the more that robot will find you just what you want.

WHAT IS RELEVANCE?

A search engine is essentially your robot—well, everyone's robot, technically—that can send you to what it deems relevant. This is how algorithmic relevance works. Since search engines get queries in the millions every split second online, it's great at predicting human behavior. That's what leads me to say relevance is important to understand when publishing books and using Amazon Advertising.

In *Amazon Keywords for Books*, I discuss how to build relevance for your publication. Building relevance comes down to a variety of factors, but the most critical factor to building relevance in the Amazon marketplace is cold, hard sales. Nothing benefits your book's relevance in the Amazon algorithm like a good old-fashioned purchase. The more sales and the more consistent those sales are, the more the algorithm trusts your product. This means you build more organic traffic and recommendations in search and with similar products.

Yes, you could get more reviews, use a social share feature on the product page, embed a sample chapter on a website, drive traffic to your product page, and so on. Those actions don't have near the same weight they used to on Amazon. Do they help? It's debatable. Will it hurt? No, but if you want the best results to build relevance in the Amazon algorithm, you must sell books.

Good news! We're talking about running Amazon ads to sell more books. The relevancy already established for your book will play a vital role in the success of your ad campaigns. The more relevant your book is to the selected targeting in an ad campaign, the less you have to spend on that targeting to get the best return on ad spend. This is where things get a little complex.

Amazon ads also have relevancy in the algorithm. Running ads isn't as simple as, "Anyone who has the most money gets the best placement across all marketplaces."

Nope. Amazon thrives on positive customer experiences. Though they understand their formula (the algorithm) isn't perfect, it's certainly user-friendly. Should a browsing customer use search and get bad recommendations, then the algorithm knows what *not* to serve you on your next search. Once someone buys your book, you build relevancy for your book in the algorithm. In the same way, once a customer interacts with your ad, the algorithm places higher relevancy on your ad.

Here's what Amazon has to say about relevancy and ads[ii]:

> *Amazon determines all of the ads with the highest relevancy. When it comes to relevancy, Amazon uses an algorithm that takes multiple factors into account to decide which ads to display. The relevancy algorithm is in place to ensure the best shopping experience for the customer.*

How can you ever build relevance on an ad that isn't running? That's where getting your product retail-ready makes the biggest difference. Simply publishing a book and praying for the best isn't a sound marketing strategy.

Let's say you use ads for your book and don't just pray for the best. You will definitely increase the odds in your favor because you have an advantage over authors who can't or don't want to use Amazon Advertising. By running campaigns, you're sending interested buyers to your product page. By sending a customer to a product they'll

WHAT IS RELEVANCE?

buy, you're increasing the relevance of your ad. The targeting used in each campaign will be where you are most relevant.

Now that you know relevance plays a huge role in book sales and Amazon Ads, you need to understand how the ads platform works. Amazon Advertising works on a virtual auction-based system where a pool of advertisers bid for specific targeting for the ad. At any moment, the algorithm doesn't search for the highest bidder like a real-world auction, but it searches for the most relevant ads.

Why?

Remember, Amazon doesn't just want your money; they want the customer's money too. If a product has a proven track record of consistent sales, then it's highly likely the algorithm is going to rule in favor of that ad. Should two products with similar relevancy compete for ad targeting, the algorithm then defaults to the highest bidder.

Things can and will change on a dime. Should the ad keep getting shown with little to no results, guess what happens to the ad? Relevance drops significantly for that ad and its targeting. The next time those two products bid against each other, the algorithm will rule in favor of the other product because the first product just wasn't pulling its weight.

In Amazon's words[iii]:

> *The auction also decides which of the most relevant ads has the highest cost-per-click (CPC) bid. A CPC bid is the maximum amount that an advertiser is willing to pay if their ad is clicked. The winner of the auction will pay an amount slightly higher than the second-highest CPC bid if their ad is clicked.*

They further go on to explain weak relevancy. Should you target the keyword "lipstick" for your Bluetooth speaker ad, you most likely won't see any results regardless of the budget or cost you affix to the ad. Since the target and the product bear little to no relevancy between the keyword and the historical search data, the algorithm deems your ad less relevant and unworthy of being shown.

Suppose you selected the keyword "audio" with your Bluetooth speaker ad, then you will have strong relevance. Therefore, your ad is more likely to display since it bears stronger relevancy. The greater the degree of ad relevancy, the higher the chances your ad will appear.

Never let that stop you from advertising. Amazon runs ads twenty-four hours a day, seven days a week. This means tons of ad space is available on the platform. Just because you don't win and get first preference doesn't mean all is lost. With all the ads served in search, on product pages, and even on third-party websites, you still have a chance of being seen. That's ultimately what marketing and promotion are for—visibility. Being seen by a new audience is better than no audience at all.

Here's the part that gets me excited each time I read it. Amazon says[iv]:

> *By advertising products that already have high sales, you're maintaining relevancy with click-through rate (CTR) and sales, helping you stay on top of mind with shoppers.*

Amazon is saying if you already have some success on their platform, they'll reward you with more customers. They know how important it is to stay top of mind for their customers. It's why quite a few people these days go to a store, check the price of an item in-store, and compare it to Amazon. This online juggernaut knows what it takes to stay top of mind and in their customer's daily life. Now, they're giving you a piece of the pie, if only you invest in their advertising.

With so many variables at play, I can't provide any one solution. But if you come back to the basic understanding of algorithmic relevance, you can make an informed decision about whether to keep advertising. When it comes to targeting in an ad, if it doesn't get a sale, it's not doing you any good.

If you've ever used the Amazon Advertising platform, you're probably going crazy because I haven't talked about cost-per-click (CPC), average cost of sales (ACoS), impressions, and all that other fancy jargon. That's for a good reason. I didn't even want to touch any of that until you've grasped relevance. Now that we're on the same page, let's push forward and get super granular with Amazon Advertising. We're going to cover the inside baseball terms, so the next time you're hanging out with some friends, you can start tossing these terms around to sound like some big-time stockbroker or cryptocurrency tycoon.

KNOWING THE TERMINOLOGY

It's not enough for you to run an ad and be done with it. You're not just paying for admission into the advertising carnival only to get a cheap prize just for playing. Nope, you must understand the details, and that all starts with five critical elements. Now, you may already know an Amazon Advertising dashboard has far more than five elements. For the sake of starting, just focus on these five elements and terms. You'll revisit these terms repeatedly throughout the book.

Once Amazon serves an ad to a customer, it sends a signal to your dashboard which is called an impression. Even though the ad *appeared* in front of a customer doesn't mean they *saw* it. Remember how I said having a killer book cover design will make or break your success in self-publishing and ads? The book cover is how you get a browsing customer's attention. When you serve the ad in front of a potential buyer, if the book cover is stellar, you should successfully deliver a pattern disrupt—meaning you stopped the customer from scrolling. In the event they don't notice your ad, don't sweat it. The best part about Amazon ads is you don't pay for impressions.

Crazy, right? On any other platform, you'll pay out the nose just to be seen by an audience who may or may not like your ad. With

Amazon, your ad appears in front of an audience you targeted. Should the customer not notice or ignore your ad, you don't pay. That's great news altogether, right? Not so fast!

Think back to the last chapter on relevancy. What do you think will happen if your ad gets served repeatedly with no actions taken by the customer? Getting no result pushes down the relevancy of an ad.

Is there a set number of impressions that'll kill relevancy? Not to my knowledge. It makes sense to assume if an ad gets tons of impressions one moment, then nothing, that ad might have worn out its welcome for that targeting. You could increase your spending, but all that'll get is a ton more impressions and possibly some negative factors.

When an ad shows to a customer, hopefully you piqued the customer's interest and got them to take action that leads to the next important metric—click. Whether clicking an ad on desktop computers or mobile, when a customer wants to learn more about a product they have seen through an ad spot, that customer's action registers as a click in your ads dashboard. Unlike impressions, you pay for clicks.

It's all fun and games until someone clicks on your ad. While getting a click can be good, it's usually an entire bag of bad. Why? Clicks are not free. Now you have to rely on the ability of your product page to convert a browsing customer into a buyer. That's why you need to get your book description written by an expert in marketing copy. Also, it doesn't hurt to focus on all the other elements like fifteen reviews, an average rating above 3.5 stars, and everything we covered previously.

What you're willing to pay for the click is where it gets interesting. Being new to the game, you probably aren't too sure what a good bid would be for a target. It truly varies based on the targeting, the demand for the targeting for both advertisers and customers, and what Amazon suggests.

Believe it or not, the suggested bid Amazon gives you isn't always the best choice. While they might tell you the average bid for a target is $1.12 to $2.02, you don't have to bid that much. As long as you bid above two cents on any target, you're good. Will you win an auction at two cents per click for a target? Not likely, but at least you're in the game.

If you bid too low on a target, then you'll know because you don't get any impressions—that means Amazon didn't even show your ad to any potentially interested customers. Some targeting requires a larger entry fee based on your relevance to the target and the competing advertisers in the virtual auction. Conversely, the more relevance your ad and product have, the cheaper the winning bid.

When you've bid for a target and a customer clicks the ad, you pay for that click based on the outcome of the auction. Cost-per-click (CPC) is how much you pay as an average for a click. As you know, the algorithm awards first preference—or prime placement—to the product and ad with the most relevance. How you bid can also affect the outcome, since your title and the competing advertiser might have relatively equal relevance for a target. Should you win an auction, you won't often pay the full amount of the bid you placed. In fact, the system is built to give authors a great deal sometimes. Once you win the auction for a target, you only pay slightly more than the second-highest bidder.[v]

For example:

- Your bid = $1.25 CPC
- Second place winner = $0.75
- Your actual CPC (what Amazon actually charges you) = $0.76

Since relevance is always fluctuating and never remains static, your actual CPC will change from one auction to the next. That's why Amazon gives the average cost-per-click for a target in your campaign dashboard. I'm not encouraging you to run your campaigns at extremely high CPCs, hoping to pay one cent above the second-highest bidder. That can be dangerous, especially if you end up getting second place in the auction.

By the way, when you get anything below first place in an auction, you still get placement. It's just not going to be in the best high-traffic areas. Your ad might end up on a Sponsored Products carousel in the sixteenth column. Though few people visit that far on the carousel, there are still some customers looking. Otherwise, Amazon wouldn't offer the option. Whatever you do, don't search for and click on your ad. It's a great way to muck up the system and slowly erode relevance of your ad. Not to mention, you'll waste your money because you'll be charged for that click—even your own.

What happens after a customer clicks on your ad? If they don't buy, is everything ruined? Not necessarily! Amazon has a fourteen-day "cookie window" where it places some trackable code with each customer. This is good *and* bad.

For one, it's good because if the customer comes back to Amazon, the website might recommend the customer visit your product page again. Yeah, Amazon saw the customer eyeing your book, but for whatever reason, they didn't buy it then. Should the customer go back to your product page and buy your book within the fourteen days after being served the ad, then that purchase will register as a sale in your ad. That's the bad part.

Did I say it's bad? Not really. The tracking has a two-week tracking delay after the initial interaction. When a customer clicks on your ad, Amazon tracks them for up to two weeks. Even though they didn't purchase your book right away, if they come back and buy it, you'll get credit for it in your dashboard. This can be particularly frustrating if you're seeing a ton of money going out, but none coming in.

Amazon Ads expert, Bryan Cohen, recommends exercising patience and using your KDP dashboard as a tool for tracking total overall sales and Kindle Unlimited page reads. Cohen further suggests using the browser extension called *Book Report* (available in the Chrome Browser Extension Store). Even though you can get all the data you want in your KDP dashboard, it's still rather unreliable for what you need at the moment. With *Book Report,* you can zero in on dates, titles, authors, and more. The purpose of tracking overall sales and results in your account is because sometimes Amazon Ads have a ripple effect across the whole account.

For instance, Amazon Advertising already has a delay in reported earnings. To compound that stress, you have customers who click an ad and might buy within those two weeks. By checking your overall sales performance, you can make an educated guess about whether an ad is effective.

The best way to monitor your performance beyond the ads dashboard is to check the period prior to your ad campaign launch. How were your sales before launching? Compare how the sales are faring with the ads. You should see a noticeable difference if your ads are performing as they should.

Whatever you do, avoid shutting off a campaign just because you think it's losing money. Analyze your data. Take your time and figure out:

1. Is the ad working?
2. What can you do to make it better?
3. What isn't working in the targeting?
4. How can you increase the good results?

Later, we'll explore the metrics you need to determine the answers to these questions. For now, put a pin in it; we'll come back to this later.

Once you have a firm grasp on the previous metrics, let's pay the closest attention to the sales and orders. The orders are the number of units sold because of your campaign. Naturally, the sales are the gross profit derived from the orders. This works in a couple of interesting ways.

First, if someone buys the book you're advertising, you'll see the retail amount paid. No, that is not your net profit, so you won't be seeing all that money. In fact, the royalty assigned to your book is what you'll make. The next way you get sales and orders is through brand-related products. Should a customer click an ad for your ebook, but purchase the print book, then you might see a higher number than usual. To my understanding, if a customer buys a book within the same series of books related to the ad, that purchase will count as a sale in the ad campaign.

You should always check the data in both your ads and KDP dashboards. Sometimes, the numbers don't paint a clear picture in your ads dashboard, so you have to do a little digging to figure out what sold.

What about organic sales? Isn't it likely the Amazon algorithm could give some love to your book? Sure, we could say organic sales will come, but think about this a bit more. What if a customer clicks on your ad, the fourteen days expire for tracking, and then they buy your book? I'd say that was a successful ad campaign. Yes, you want to have almost immediate success with your ads. Still, you shouldn't overlook the power of long-term success using ads.

Customers have varying reasons they might not buy right now. Maybe they don't have the money. They could be in a position where your book isn't quite what they needed yet. Though book sales come naturally without ads, I wouldn't bank on them unless you're already raking in the sales. In that case, the ads are only going to further push your relevance in the Amazon marketplace.

The next metric to pay close attention to is KENP read (also known as Kindle Edition Normalized Page). KENP is a metric for anyone who enrolls their ebook into the KDP Select Program. This exclusivity agreement allows your ebook to land in the Kindle Unlimited library where patrons pay a monthly fee to Amazon in exchange for reading as much content as they wish. For every page read, the author gets paid less than half a cent. If you have an ebook enrolled in KDP Select and are running ads to that book, then Amazon Advertising tracks the pages read. This is neat, because you might see no sales, but might see actual pages read.

Half a cent isn't anything that'll make you rich overnight, but it's better in a different way. Anytime a Kindle Unlimited member checks out your ebook, Amazon registers it as a quasi-sale. Though you aren't getting paid the same, you'll get the same love from the Amazon algorithm as if it were a sale. In fact, so much so that your title can become a number one bestseller in its given category without selling a single book. If you have a series and drive traffic to the first book, then imagine what the readthrough will be! While an ad might eat up your money, you could still see KENP readthrough in your series. What the ads dashboard does *not* track is the readthrough or the customer checking out additional books in the Kindle Unlimited program as part of a series.

Remember how I said it was important to track all data in both dashboards? This is why! Your ads will have a compounding effect across your whole catalog. This is good news for you prolific authors. If you did the hard work upfront and created binge-worthy content, then running ads for a book is a simple decision. You can even run an ad that's a loss leader. Its sole function is to bring customers into your universe. While you may lose money up front because you're advertising to customers who don't click and buy your book, the backend page reads and readthrough will make up the difference.

Finally, the last item for us to cover is the daily budget, the amount you're willing to invest every day. While you can budget your daily spend to $1, Amazon recommends you set it to $10 or greater for the best results.

I've run ad campaigns at $1 a day and seen sales, but it's nothing monumental. With such a low budget, Amazon is less apt to serve your ad to customers for fear of blowing through your budget, especially if your CPC is high.

For instance, if you set a daily budget at $1 a day and your default CPC bid is $0.50, then you only have enough money to get two clicks per day. After those two clicks, your ad gets paused until the next day. Getting your ad paused isn't the end of the world but it can be counter-productive in building relevance for your ad. How can the algorithm build trust and place relevancy in your ad if it's not live 24/7?

On the opposite side of the spectrum, placing a daily budget beyond your means isn't the best idea. You shouldn't invest more than you can stand to lose or afford. Jacking up your ad spend without having the funds is never a good idea either. Sure, you might get a bunch of sales, but then what? The money from the sales won't hit your bank account for another sixty days or so. With Amazon Advertising, they bill you right away and in a couple of different ways.

If you're new to the Amazon Advertising platform, then you'll have to pay in tiered increments. They first ping your preferred billing method with a fractional amount. This merely confirms you have a legitimate payment method. From there, Amazon Advertising bills according to these increments until you've hit the top threshold. After you hit the top threshold, you'll simply get billed at the beginning of every calendar month. The billing tiers include[vi]:

1. $50
2. $150
3. $200
4. $350
5. $500

Should you exceed the credit limit, Amazon will charge you more than once a month. That's not saying they'll double bill you, but instead you'll pay as you go. I stress caution around budgeting properly again. Don't run ads unless you have the money to pay right away. It can get real ugly real quick if you're essentially borrowing money from Amazon to run ads.

For payments that are rejected, Amazon Advertising will pause all your campaigns and hold your account hostage until you can square away the past due amount. I made the mistake once of leaving a credit card on file that was going to expire. When it expired, I got an email from Amazon telling me the issue. Naturally, I resolved the problem, but when I turned my ads back on, they lost a *lot* of their previous momentum. Don't forget to occasionally double-check your payment method so you don't screw up any momentum like I did.

The next biggest issue with daily budgets is sometimes you simply won't spend that much. In fact, Amazon states[vii]:

You may spend less than your daily budget, or up to 10% more than your daily budget. This helps you benefit from high-traffic days.

This is Amazon's way of warning that you could be severely under budget and, sometimes, 10% over budget. I haven't had any issues with going over budget, but I'm sure there's a first time for everything. To avoid any issues, I recommend checking your ads daily. No, you don't have to monitor your ads multiple times per day. Check once every day at the same time, so you have an accurate idea of where your ad spend is.

Just remember to have patience when running your ads, cross-check the ads dashboard with your KDP sales dashboard (or *Book Report*), and adjust your ads only when necessary. According to Amazon, it can take up to seventy-two hours to complete traffic validation[viii]. While your ads dashboard might say you have no sales from an ad, your KDP dashboard might say otherwise. Then, three days later, the ads dashboard will catch up.

Using the ads dashboard alone is a recipe for disaster. In due time, Amazon will tighten up the real-time reporting and give a more accurate idea of your spend-to-sales ratio. Even then, it's hard to predict if a customer will buy your book within the fourteen-day cookie window. That's understandable and rather nice. We get the benefit of tracking fourteen days out. All we have to do is sit back and wait. It's not the best feeling when you see your ad burning money while pulling in no sales. Given time, you'll see those sales come in.

What you shouldn't do is go to the extreme and think you can blow through thousands in ad spend in a day with zero sales. There's a ton of risk and little reward if you're waiting for your sales to drop in. That's why checking your actual sales will give you an idea of what is working.

While there are tons of other terms in Amazon Advertising, I'm going to save those for future chapters. Amazon is constantly updating the features and options in the dashboard, but the fundamentals usually remain. We've covered the basic terminology you'll need to know.

Now that we have focused on the terms, let's get a broader view of the ads, how they function, and what works best for your books.

WHAT ADS FUNCTION BEST FOR BOOKS?

B ased on the catchy title, you probably skipped to this chapter hoping to get an answer to this question. If you breezed past the previous chapters, you're missing a lot. Go back and read those sections first. Otherwise, what I'll share will be hazy and possibly confusing.

You have three ad types you can use, with some regional exceptions. The two ads I prefer are Sponsored Product and Sponsored Brand ads. I'm not fond of the third option, Lockscreen Ads, as you'll soon discover. For now, let's focus on Sponsored Product and Brand ads.

SPONSORED PRODUCT ADS RULE!

I wouldn't mind if all you ever did was run Sponsored Product ads. They're simple to set up, can be as relatively cheap (or as expensive) as you like, and you can learn a lot by setting up a few of these ad types. Using **Sponsored Product** ads yields me a high return on investment, and you'll find out my exact process here.

When you run a Sponsored Product ad, Amazon serves your book in a variety of places, including:

- Product pages related to your book
- In search queries
- On third-party sites

For product page placement, you'll typically find an image carousel with the title **Products related to this item,** followed by a smaller size **Sponsored** tag. I'm sure by the time I publish this book, they'll change the name again. The common denominator every time is the **Sponsored** tag. Any time you see a product image, look for that tag and you'll know an advertiser paid for the space. Naturally, the better the placement is, the more algorithmically relevant the ad is to the customer.

PRODUCT PAGES RELATED TO YOUR BOOK

The first type of ad placement is on relevant product pages. You'll typically find the ad carousel on a browser just below the book description, right beneath the From the Publisher and Editorial Reviews section, or just below the Author Bio section. Amazon constantly split tests for various placements of the carousel, so there's no hard and fast rule for ad carousel placement.

You can find out if you had first position placement in your ads reports. Getting the first spot can make a *huge* difference in conversions. However, just because you get first position placement doesn't mean people will buy your book.

Should you get first position placement but don't convert a sale after a certain number of clicks, reconsider your:

1. **Targeting.** You may not be targeting the right keyword, category, or product. That's okay. Simply pause the targeting

and possibly use it as a negative target. More on negative keywords and products later.

2. **Book Description.** This seems rather redundant, but it bears repeating. If you're driving traffic to your product page and you aren't closing the deal, then your ad copy needs work.

IN SEARCH QUERIES

Any time a customer uses the search bar feature, Amazon provides a set of products tailored to their prior browsing and buying history. Self-publishing expert Dave Chesson shared insights on the best spots to convert a sale on Amazon and it starts with the first position placement[ix]. The first product served is often the product customers are most likely to buy. However, Dave's case study focused on organic search results and not Amazon ads.

Sponsored Product ads get prime placement right above the first organic search result. Having this placement can make a tremendous difference in the traffic, clicks, and sales your ad gets. The tough part of it all is you're going to have to qualify for the winning bid by:

- Having the most relevance for your product among other advertisers; and
- Outbidding other products with similar relevancy

What if you don't get first position placement for your ad? Does that mean your ads won't be effective? Not necessarily. Just because you didn't win the auction for a targeting bid doesn't mean customers won't see your ad. You'll just have to realize your odds of a sale diminish the further down the ads pecking order you are.

Of course, there is a silver lining in all this. Should you *not* get the winning bid, you'll at least pay how much you bid or less, so long as you kept the bidding fixed or bidding dynamic down. Later, you'll learn more about that feature once we dive deeper into running a Sponsored Product ad.

The biggest perk, by far, of using Sponsored Product ads is how seamlessly integrated the ad is in the search volume. Most customers outside the self-publishing business aren't even aware the ad is, in fact, an ad. It just seems like an integral part of the search results.

When a customer does a search query on Amazon, they'll get sixteen organic results with a handful of ads sprinkled throughout, including the Sponsored Brand banner at the top of the search. Stay with me, we'll get to Sponsored Brand ads soon.

SPONSORED BRAND AD—BANNERS FOR YOUR BRAND

Most newbies should skip using Sponsored Brand ads because it requires having multiple publications to advertise. For prolific authors, Sponsored Brand ads could be for you. What makes these ads so enticing is the placement and the appearance.

When running a Sponsored Brand ad, you get placement at the top of the search results. Outside of that, you won't see this ad placement. According to Amazon, they believe you "help shoppers discover your brand and products…with rich, engaging creatives."

To be less ambiguous, your ad is a banner at the top of search results that displays:

- **Your brand logo.** So, you'll need to provide your logo.

- **Custom headline.** Good copywriting will make the most of this space.
- **Up to 3 products.** You can select 3 books from your author catalog.

Though three is the minimum number of products for a banner ad, Amazon encourages you to add at least five products. As mentioned previously, in the event your product is out of stock or unavailable, Amazon pauses your ad, and you lose all momentum you previously built. Again, this doesn't happen often and usually affects print-on-demand books published away from KDP.

More recently, Amazon Ads rolled out Sponsored Brand ads that direct customers to your Author Central Profile, which provides access to your entire catalog. The jury is still out on this new feature, but I'm cautiously optimistic.

When a customer clicks on your banner ad, they'll go to a special landing page with your featured products. You can preview how the landing page will look for the customer during ad set up. Normally, the first product you pick will have a spotlight in the middle of the landing page. All the other products will be above it with less emphasis. Your products are still clickable and give your potential buyer opportunities to buy your books.

With Sponsored Brand ads, I get more clicks with fewer conversions than with Sponsored Product ads. I've often theorized the targeting could be wrong or the ad copy might be subpar. I've used the same targeting on a successful Sponsored Product ad and got better results. That's not to say you shouldn't try Sponsored Brand ads. I'm simply warning you of the potential dangers of using this ad type. Be prepared to pay more for this placement.

I only recommend using Sponsored Brands if you're an established author with a deep back catalog and you have the discretionary expense to test this ad type.

Oh, and one thing that bothers me is you do not get automatic targeting as you do in Sponsored Product ads. In the Amazon Advertising Certification Courses, they suggest breaking into ads using automatic targeting. Once an ad gets traction, then you can scrape all the data and create a new ad with manual targeting.

With Sponsored Product ads, you're left to sift your way through the best targeting and have to figure it out on your own. Maybe I am a bit too reliant on automatic targeting ads, but it sure is nice having Amazon do the work for me and remove as much guesswork as possible.

For whatever reservations I had with Sponsored Brand banners, I'm nowhere near as reluctant about them as Lockscreen Ads. That leads me to my next point…

LOCKSCREEN ADS: THEY'RE A MONEY PIT

When some Amazon readers turn on their Kindle e-Reader or Fire Tablet, they'll see an ad first. Amazon sells two different e-readers and tablets—ad-supported or ad-free. To get an ad-free experience, customers have to pay more. Naturally, everyone wants to save money, even if it's saving a few bucks. Having an ad-supported device means the customer has one hoop to jump through on the way to reading.

First, they turn on the device. An ad will appear for a book, and it's usually based on their buying or browsing history on Amazon. In theory, the ads should focus on the customer's interests. What I've noticed is often the complete opposite. When I open my Kindle Paperwhite or Fire HD 10 Tablet, I usually get an ad for something altogether uninteresting to me.

For the tablet, it's not surprising that not all ads are for books. On Kindle though, you'll get nothing but book ads. The advertisers are naturally traditional publishing companies or self-published authors. Unless these advertisers didn't choose the right targeting, I found 90% of the time my ads are for romance novels. For the record, I'm not opposed to the romance niche, but I can assure you I spend no time reading romance these days.

My wife made the argument that we have a connected account. Since she reads romance, it's quite possible she tainted my reading history. Therefore, advertisers are paying for ad space on the wrong Kindle reader.

Here's the real kicker, and why I don't endorse Lockscreen Ads. The ad prevents readers from doing what they came to do—read what they bought already. In my opinion, rather than fuss with it, much less pay attention to it, most readers swipe to remove the ad and move on.

Even though the Kindle e-Reader is now over a decade old, the technology isn't advanced enough yet to expect a single swipe to open the device efficiently. When my e-reader is slow to open, I sometimes get impatient and swipe again or tap the ad by accident. My apologies to the advertisers out there who spent money on my impatience, but it's true. If I'm making this little mistake, can you imagine how many other customers are doing it too?

With Sponsored Products and Sponsored Brands, the audience is warm already. Customers come to Amazon to browse products and potentially spend money. With Lockscreen Ads, the customer has already invested in a book and isn't as receptive to the ads. I'm sure I can speak for other readers out there when I say—when I open a book, that's the only thing I want to worry about. I spent my money already; wasn't that enough?!

Amazon also places Lockscreen ads on the bottom of the Kindle Home Screen. I accidentally tap on those placements occasionally. The placement isn't terrible here. I imagine it's less disruptive than the screen-based version. Customers might be a little more open to buying another book, so long as they're not forced into getting past it to read their current catalog.

Lockscreen ads gobble up every bit of your daily budget. To make matters worse, your ad could reach the wrong customer altogether. You're probably thinking you could simply stick with specific keywords or products. Of course, that's not at all true. These ad types only have interest-based targeting. You select the category you believe your book best fits. Keep in mind that when you choose a single category with any ad type, you're asking Amazon to place your ad on any book in that given category. Selecting one category might be enough.

Before you run a Lockscreen Ad, make sure you study the categories by doing a quick search on Amazon using the category keyword. Does your book fit the search volume? If so, go for it. If the search query returns a bunch of unrelated books, avoid that category.

Lockscreen Ads are not for the faint of heart! Between the broad category-based targeting and the disruptive nature of the ad placement, matters only become worse when you realize you have to provide the ad copy and set a lifetime budget. You'll learn more practical steps in a future chapter on this setup. However, I'll be the last person to teach you anything about ad copy, so just understand you're on your own in that department. I highly recommend reading Brian Meeks' *Mastering Amazon Descriptions* where he explains copywriting fundamentals. Simply take what you learn about descriptions and apply that to your ad copy.

The **Lifetime budget** is where you should pay closest attention. With other ad types, you can set a start and end date even while allowing the campaign to run indefinitely. Lockscreen ads only allow for a start and end date with no continuous running feature. If you want a Lockscreen ad to continue running, adjust the end date yourself. Good luck, because if you don't catch that end date before it's over, that ad is toast! That's especially painful when you have a Lockscreen Ad taking off.

The budget also functions differently. Rather than looking at daily ad spend, you get a **Lifetime budget**. This means you're willing to spend up to this amount (your set **Lifetime budget**). Of course, this comes with the same guarantee as the other ad types in which Amazon says they'll spend up to or 10% above your budget.

Making matters worse is the pacing option for your **Lifetime budget**. You can choose to run the campaign as quickly as possible or spread the campaign evenly during your set time. When spending as quickly as possible, you can imagine how fast a budget goes, especially if you set the CPC high. However, Amazon shies away from lower lifetime budgets with low CPCs that are set on evenly spread campaigns. Why? Amazon can stretch this amount without going over your budget in the set time frame.

The minimum ad spend for **Lockscreen ads** is $100. If you do the math, you'll see that translates to spending $3.33 per day during a 30-day campaign. Yikes! That's an incredibly low daily budget. The good news is you can increase your budget while the campaign runs. Be careful though; once you increase the budget, you cannot decrease it. Should you accidentally increase the spend and cannot afford it, simply pause the campaign and start a new one if you still have the money.

Overall, **Lockscreen Ads** need more options and flexibility before I wholeheartedly endorse them. While I can show you how to set up a campaign, I don't use them myself. Should you have a bigger ads budget, then try it out. If you're publishing romance, chances are likely I'm going to see your ad at some point. I'll do my best *not* to click on it.

HOW TO SET UP & MANAGE AN AMAZON AD

Amazon Advertising isn't simply plug-and-play, nor can you expect to get significant results by blindly following directions from anyone. It's going to take time, patience, and a deeper understanding of how the ads platform functions.

If you're ready to rock and roll, then let's jump into the practical application of setting up and managing an ad. While some of what I explain will be a brief review, most of what you'll learn is the specific items you should pay closest attention to and why.

Naturally, I'm going to lean into my favorite ad type: Sponsored Product ads. Rather than repeat information from that setup in the subsequent ad types, I trust you'll read through everything *before* firing off any ad campaign. Again, understanding the basics will clear up any ambiguity and will make you a bit more confident in your approach.

The next ad type you'll tap into is the Sponsored Brand banner ad. Again, I highly recommend only experienced authors with a deeper budget use this option. It can become costly, and if you don't have enough of a backlog of books, things could get ugly real fast!

Even though I'm not the biggest proponent of Lockscreen Ads, I'll still discuss how to set those up and manage them. If this section seems brief, then it's for good reason. I simply don't like Lockscreen Ads nor see much use for them until Amazon can:

a) Roll out the same targeting as the other ad types
b) Make this ad type available in all regions, not just the U.S.
c) Allow for more flexibility in what the author shares on-screen

Amazon favors traditionally published authors versus self-published authors. The Lockscreen ads for traditionally published books are more eye-catching and have so much more versatility to them. For self-published books? Not so much. Amazon essentially implies through their preferential treatment: *You don't like it? We don't care.* It's harsh, but true. Let's get into it!

SETTING UP A SPONSORED PRODUCT AD

Before you can run any ads, set up your billing profile. Supply Amazon with a form of payment and double-check your form of payment to ensure it has the proper funds to run campaigns. Remember the tiered levels of billing Amazon puts your account through; expect multiple billings as your ads grow.

Should you make it your goal to burn through every credit tier so you switch to monthly billing? No, just let it play out and be ready to get billed a few times in a month if you're ambitious with your budget.

Visit your dashboard and click the yellow **Create campaign** button to get things going. You'll see the three options you need to get started. Next, select the **Continue** button on the **Sponsored Product**

ads option to begin your first ad. With all ads, you must come up with a naming sequence of sorts. Meaning, you want to name each campaign so that you know what it is at a glance. For me, I simply create an abbreviation or a short keyword for a book, then the version, ad type, plus the date.

For example, if I'm running an automated targeting campaign for my book *Amazon Keywords for Books*, then the Campaign name would look something like this:

Keywords v1 AUTO 071024

You do not have to use my system for naming your campaign. Go with what makes the most sense to you. Can you see elements like the ad type, book, and date in the ads dashboard? Sure, but you'll identify what you're looking for a lot faster with a naming scheme.

The next option is the Portfolio drop-down menu. Portfolios are an easy way to organize your ads into folders. Having similar brands and authors in one portfolio helps you analyze the overall performance of your ads rather than simply one ad set at a time.

> Sadly, assuming this is your first time using Amazon Ads, setting up a Portfolio may not be necessary. In fact, you'll have to set up the Portfolio in your main dashboard and cannot establish it in the ads set up.
>
> Just in case you need that short tutorial, here it is:
>
> 1. In your main dashboard, under the **Management** tab, select the option to **+ Create a portfolio**.

2. Name your campaign based on the author name, brand, series of books, or however you plan to organize it.
3. Click the **Create a portfolio** button.
4. Now, create a campaign or add any existing campaigns.

The rest is fairly intuitive. Once you have a Portfolio set with many campaigns, you can view your ads at a glance and adjust settings across all the campaigns. Good luck!

Now, set a start and end date for your campaign. Rather than thinking about it from the date standpoint, I want you to focus on your total budget. How much can you afford to spend within a time frame? Obviously, the higher the budget, the longer the campaign you can make and the more you can spend in a set timeline.

For me, I set my ad without an end date. I monitor my ads frequently and have the discretionary budget to afford occasional overspending. If you know you only have $100 to spend on your book for the next month, then set your end date for one month out. Should you find you are way under budget, as that happens more than you know, you can always edit your campaign and adjust the end date or put it to no end date. There's zero pressure.

I heard a theory about setting the end date thirty days out at a time. The thought was by having an end date, Amazon feels a sense of urgency to serve your ad. This simply isn't true. I tested this theory many times and found campaigns with and without a date performed exactly the same. Furthermore, authors had to keep moving the end date out once the initial month ended. This creates way too much work for an already complex process. Just don't do this. It's a waste of precious time.

Not to mention if you put an end date on your campaign and arrive on the date, the ad gets shut off. There's no turning the ad back on, hoping to gain any momentum back in your favor. Rather than ruin your chances of a successful ad campaign, build the discipline to monitor your ads regularly, then set **No end date**.

If you ever want to end a campaign before the set end date, you can. There's no pressure to keep running a campaign despite what you originally set. I remember jumping into ads originally and feeling obligated to fulfill my timeline. In fact, you could set up an ad one second, get approved, then pause or end that same campaign in the next second. There are no extra charges, and you only have to pay for the clicks on the ad while collecting any earnings you made during the campaign.

Now comes the **Daily Budget**, where you set the budget you wish to stay at or below. Amazon will spend no more than 10% above your budget or below the set budget. Full disclosure: I've never had an ad go over budget. Ever. I've run hundreds of ads the past few years, so you can breathe a sigh of relief. However, you should know that they state the possibility of an overage. Build that overage into your budget to be safe. Assuming you only have $110 to spend per day, you'll set your daily budget at $100 instead. The extra $10 is in case Amazon overspends.

Should you spend under your daily budget, reallocate the additional spend to another day. Amazon even states:

If the campaign spends less than your daily budget, the leftover amount can be used to increase your daily budget up to 25% on other days of the calendar month.

That's kind of cool considering you already have the money, but Amazon wasn't using it. So, you might as well use it on a day when you're getting a larger number of customers and traffic.

In the past, Amazon recommended setting your daily budget at or above $10 per day. While I don't know their reason for this arbitrary number, it makes sense if your CPC is rather high. Keep in mind, if your daily budget is the absolute minimum of $1 per day and your CPC is $0.30, then you'll only be able to get 3-4 clicks per day. That's simply not enough to get solid and reliable results.

I typically start any campaign at $10 and gradually increase that amount as the campaign performs better and better. Whereas if the campaign isn't performing too well, I'll kick back that daily ad spend. However, I cannot think of any time when I had to walk back a $10 per-day ad budget. Usually, once an ad takes off, I kick it up. Sometimes, the ad will lose momentum and begin burning a hole in my bank account. In that case, I'll decrease the daily budget.

Start with what you can reasonably afford and increase when you can swing it. If you can only start with $1 per day, then so be it. I often tell my clients that at $1 per day, you're paying to learn the Amazon Ads platform. Any sale you make in the process is gravy.

Now that you have the basic setup started, we're going to deviate a bit into different ad types in Automatic and Manual targeting.

UNDERSTANDING AUTOMATIC TARGETING FOR SPONSORED PRODUCT ADS

With Automatic Targeting, you're allowing Amazon to take the wheel. I used to believe it was a recipe for disaster, giving the steering wheel to a company that benefits directly from running your ads.

Can you trust Amazon not to blow through your money without results? Actually, yes. You can.

Remember, Amazon is in the business of making their customers happy. Even though you might think of yourself as a vendor, you are, in fact, a customer of Amazon Advertising. This means Amazon views you as a customer and wants the best possible outcome for everyone involved.

With that said, running **Automatic Targeting** (aka auto ads) doesn't mean you should just plug and play. You still have to manage the ad, collect data, and adjust any targeting where necessary.

In the *Amazon Advertising Certification Course*, you learn how Amazon believes the best place for any advertiser to start is auto ads. The reason for this is because your ad appears in front of customers through relevant or related products, keywords, or categories. Amazon looks at your book, the sales history, and the metadata to determine the best fit. That's not to say their targeting is perfect, but it at least takes all the guesswork out of it for you.

As the ad goes out, you'll see what targeting converts the sale and what doesn't. The next step is to extrapolate the info, refine the ad, and build out new manual targeting ads based on the sales converting targets and negative targets. Where you see a sale occurring, you'll want to use that targeting again in other ad sets. Whereas if a specific target is burning through your budget, you can add it to your negative targeting.

Before you ever get to that, let's set up the rest of your ad…

SETTING A CAMPAIGN BIDDING STRATEGY

Advertisers often misunderstand the next section of the **Campaign Bidding Strategy**. It creates a ton of confusion for newbies. If you don't get this section right, you could either spend well over your desired cost-per-click (CPC), therefore burning through your budget, or you might severely underspend and get no results from your ad.

You have three choices:

1. Dynamic bids down
2. Dynamic bids up and down
3. Fixed bids

I almost always recommend using dynamic bids down only because Amazon has your best interests at heart. Should your ad be less likely to convert a sale, Amazon will lower your bid in real time. This comes back to the relevancy of your product and the ad. Should they see your book isn't converting for specific targeting or that prime placement never gets a sale, they'll drop your bid.

How much? Enough that you're not spending the full CPC set for the targeting.

Dynamic bids up and down are for advertisers with a deeper budget and a higher risk threshold. While this bidding strategy includes the real time bidding down option in cases of lower conversion, it also includes the exact opposite. Should Amazon view your product and ad as more likely to convert a sale, they'll increase your bid up to 100% above CPC. This can be disastrous if you aren't careful. Just because they think your ad is likely to convert a sale doesn't mean it will.

For **Fixed bids**, Amazon won't mess with your CPC at all. If your bid is at $0.50 CPC, then they won't spend beyond that. Can you still pay less for a click? Sure! Remember, the winning bidder sets the actual cost-per-click for everyone.

Let's say I bid $0.50, but I'm the third or fourth place winning bid. Amazon looks at the winning bidder, adjusts their bid one cent above the second-highest winning bid, then everyone follows suit behind. In the event the second-place winning bid was $0.40, then the first-place winner pays $0.41 while the rest of the bids adjust below the $0.40. Even though I might have bid $0.10 above the second-highest bid, my bid is going to adjust behind them. Pretty cool, right?

On the opposite side of things, if the second-highest bid is at $0.60, then most likely your cost will default back to your $0.50 bid.

Do I recommend fixed bids? Sure, if you don't want Amazon to fuss with your ad and adjust placement according to how they feel the ad will convert. Before you do that, I want you to consider why Amazon would suppress your ad based on conversions. Remember, their focus is on the best interests of both customers: the advertiser and the browsing customer. Rather than show your ad to someone less likely to buy, they'll drop that bid a bit for more prime real estate in front of the right customer. I'm going to lean in favor of **Dynamic bids—down only** so I mitigate any unnecessary spend.

Speaking of adjusting bids, now comes the part where your ad spend could go through the roof if you aren't careful—**Adjust bids by placement (replaces Bid+)**. This drop-down option is only for the experienced advertiser and anyone using it should do so with caution.

As you might assume, bidding a specific percentage above for special placement is how this option functions. First, you can get first-page placement. Based on the percentage you select, you're agreeing to pay that much more for your CPC if you get the top of the first page.

The next option for adjusted bids is for product page placement. As you're aware, product pages have a carousel. Landing on that carousel in a suitable spot isn't a given, especially if you're competing against other similarly relevant books. Rather than mess around as you would in a real-world auction, this bidding strategy allows you to cut to the front of the line with your absolute highest CPC.

You can increase your bids upwards of 900%. Let's do the math on this one. If you have your CPC set at $0.10 and set your adjusted bid for **Top-of-search** or **Product** pages, then that amount would be $0.90. Ouch! That could really hurt your daily budget, but it could be worthwhile if it converts a sale.

For me, I rarely use the adjust bids function because I saw some rather unspectacular results from using it. The few times I used it were when I was building a tier two or greater ad. Meaning, I'd run an ad, scrape the data, and build another ad based on the first. With every campaign you build, you'll find targeting that converts really well. If you know beyond a shadow of a doubt that your book sells with specific targeting, then use the adjust bids option.

Just a quick word about your ad strategy, because it's easy to get carried away trying to use every feature and option right away. Be careful about continually changing your ad strategy during a campaign; it can lead to disaster.

SELECTING THE AD FORMAT

Right now, this feature is exclusive to Amazon U.S. and is available in no other regions. You either select **Custom text ad** or **Standard ad**. With custom text ads, you have 150 characters or fewer to develop ad copy that closes the deal. When you select the custom ad option and the book you wish to advertise, scroll down to the bottom of the setup window to see the Ad preview and the custom text box.

Amazon Advertising has very strict rules and guidelines to follow when using custom text. I recommend a few things:

- Avoid all caps
- It's not a headline, so capitalize only the first word in the sentence
- Don't make outrageous claims (i.e., lose 50 pounds in the next week)
- Avoid pricing information

Again, Amazon Advertising has an entire laundry list of demands, so cross-check their guidelines before running your first custom text ad. Custom ads are nice and some self-publishers swear by them. However, I have noticed no actual difference in conversion rates from custom text ads and standard ads. Then again, I'm not a copywriting expert, so chances are likely my custom ads perform just as well as my standard ads because my ad copy isn't good.

It's rather telling if you think about it. In regions like the UK, Canada, and Australia, advertisers run highly successful campaigns without having to dial in ad copy. I had access to the Amazon Advertising dashboard through the Amazon Advantage program long before they rolled out access to regions outside the U.S. I found they never had custom text, so it's rather suspect how Amazon didn't roll out custom text ads with the recent access to non-U.S. regions.

Will they expand custom text ads to the other regions? Possibly, but I can't predict that, and Amazon Advertising reps haven't shared inside intel.

When selecting the **Custom text ad** option, you'll notice the ad copy box when you scroll all the way to the bottom of the ad set up. Whereas with standard ads, you'll get another choice just below it called **Create an Ad Group**. When you plan to launch multiple campaigns with the same set of targeting and products, this allows you to run them all under one group. This makes for efficient management, especially when you want to suppress irrelevant targets through the negative targeting feature.

For instance, when you find specific targeting that performs very low for your brand, you can find that out in your **Search Terms** report and drop the targeting into the **Negative keyword** or **Product targeting**. Then, that change is applied to all campaigns in the group, essentially saving you time.

Sadly, when choosing the custom text option, you won't have the benefit of creating an ad group. This requires a little more work and time.

When creating an ad group, use the same system of naming your group as you do your ad campaign. Stick to something you'll know at a glance, so it saves you time and avoids any confusion when you're running dozens of campaigns at a time.

SELECTING YOUR PRODUCT FOR AN AUTOMATIC TARGETING CAMPAIGN

Since your KDP account integrates with your Amazon Advertising account, your entire collection of books should appear in the Products area. The display window scrolls down, showing all your books. To make matters easy, you can simply type in the book's title you wish to advertise. Immediately, you will see the cover, hyperlinked title, average star rating, number of reviews, the price, the ASIN, and if it's in stock or out of stock.

In the event you're publishing to Amazon—accessing Amazon Advertising through Author Central or a seller account—you'll need your book's ASIN or ISBN. Simply search for your book, and they'll give you the option to advertise your selection.

Naturally, there's nothing you can do if the product lists as out of stock. Don't bother running a campaign on a product that's not in stock. If you believe there is an error, visit your KDP dashboard, scroll to the bottom, and click the **Contact Us** feature. The rest is intuitive. You essentially want to find out why your book is out of stock and what you can do to resolve the issue.

For the other publishing platforms outside of KDP, you'll have to contact the print-on-demand company you're using (i.e., IngramSpark, Draft2Digital, Lulu, etc.). In most instances, it always falls back on Amazon, yet they'll never cop to it. Be prepared for circular communication when you're looking for answers to the out-of-stock problem.

You can advertise multiple books in one ad by simply clicking the **Add** button for the title you wish to use. I discourage advertising multiple books on one ad because it can get messy and it is much harder to manage the campaign. Stick with one title at a time. If you must advertise multiple books, then consider listing the ebook, paperback, or hardcover version of the same book.

Though you might have a series that has related targeting, it's best to split test what works for one book over the other. If you have to choose to advertise one book over another because of a low budget, stick with the first in a series. Should your first book in a series hook your new readers, they'll buy or check out the next book. It doesn't cost you a dime after the one time the customer clicked your ad and got your book.

SETTING THE BID FOR AN AUTOMATIC TARGETING AD

In the next section, you'll set the default bid or adjust bidding based on the type of targeting. Both have pros and cons, but remember, you can change your bidding strategy as you go.

Amazon Advertising sets the default bid at $0.75. Adjust this to what makes the most sense for your budget and goals. Remember, not everyone who clicks your ad will buy your book. In fact, you'll see a conversion rate that could be around one sale out of every twenty clicks. That's just a general estimate. Your results can be worse or way better.

When starting out, think about the royalty you make per book. Then, figure out how many clicks you can make from that profit. Here's an example:

- Your book = $14.99
- Your royalty earned per sale = $3.85
- Your bid = $0.38

- Total clicks = 10
- Total spend = $3.80

What if you don't convert a sale in ten clicks? Well, you're clearly going to be in the hole and out of money, but sometimes, that's necessary to get truly valuable data about the ad. Often, you'll find ads that function into the red well before going into the black. That's why you need to monitor regularly to make sure you're not losing your tail.

Based on the previous example, if you convert one out of every ten clicks, then you will at least break even on the ad. Don't forget about one very important part of advertising—buythrough. If you send customers to the first in a series of books or one of your brand's books, then if that customer likes the first book, they'll likely purchase more. The rising tide raises all boats.

That's a huge reason you shouldn't simply limit your data analysis to the Amazon Ads dashboard. Browser plug-ins like Book Report help clear up the confusion and give you a better overhead view of how advertising affects your entire backlog of books.

Side note: I don't recommend relying on the KDP Reports tab because it's sometimes wonky and unreliable. I'm sure this instability comes from recent changes and updates to their user interface. It's likely at some point KDP Reports will be much more reliable. Until then, I suggest using Book Report.

You will notice something across all of the bidding for specific targets—a suggested bid. I used to be wholeheartedly against the suggested bid since it felt like Amazon was merely looking to pull more money from me. The thing is, they are only sharing data based on what other advertisers are bidding for the same targeting as a whole.

You'll typically see a suggested bid along with a range. This number reflects what advertisers are bidding and where you might fit in. Do you have to use the suggested bid? No, but if the number is reasonable, go for it.

In setting up an automatic targeting campaign for my book *Amazon Keywords for Books*, my suggested bid is $0.69, with a suggested bid range of $0.52 to $1.01. Wow! Can you imagine bidding a buck for targeting? That's crazy, right? Well, not entirely so.

Just because you bid an amount doesn't mean you'll pay that much. If you kept your bids as dynamic down only, you won't spend beyond your bid. Should you not win the auction, your bid will only follow suit with the others. If the winning bid was $0.75 and the second winning bid was $0.50, then the winner only pays $0.51, and you'd be below that amount since you don't get top priority.

Breathe a sigh of relief knowing you can set your bid however you wish. Should the ad stall out or not perform at all, you can increase it later. I strongly encourage setting it at a reasonable price. If you don't have a deep backlog of books or a full series, then it may not make sense for you to bid $1 per click. You'll burn through your budget quickly and be left worrying over your conversion rate. After all, if you're profiting $3 per sale and your bid is $1 per click, then you better darn well be converting at least one out of every three clicks.

Before setting your default bid, understand that not all bids are equal in an automatic targeting ad. In fact, the next option in this section is **Set bids by targeting group**. With four different targeting groups, you'll take a different approach to bidding.

Selecting the default bid places the same bid across all four targeting groups of Close match, Loose match, Substitutes, and Complements. You'll also notice the suggested bid is slightly different because of each target.

For **Close match**, Amazon serves your ad to shoppers who use search terms closely related to your book. If your book is *The Home Exercise Plan*, then Amazon may serve your ad to customers who search "home exercise" or "exercise plan."

With **Loose match**, Amazon shows your ad to shoppers who use search terms loosely related to your book. For instance, if your book is *The Home Exercise Plan*, then Amazon may serve your ad to searches like "home planning" or "computer exercises." While these aren't the best keywords to associate with your brand, it's certainly worth trying. For loose match, I keep the bids low since the relevancy is likely to be low. It's still worth a shot. Should I find my budget getting burned rather quick, I pause this target.

The next option is **Substitutes** where Amazon shows ads on product pages similar to yours. Assuming your book is still *The Home Exercise Plan,* chances are likely your ad will appear on product pages with home exercise plans on it. I like this option and will often bid more on it since Amazon serves that ad in front of a warmer, more receptive audience.

For the last option, **Complements**, your ad will appear on product pages that complement your book. Though this is a rough example, I'll share anyway. Your example of *The Home Exercise Plan* might appear on exercise equipment and products related to home exercise. This option is another nice feature since you're, again, appearing in front of the exact audience you want to buy your book.

Keep in mind, you don't have to use all four options. In fact, you can pause the option you don't want by clicking the switch off. If it's gray, it's off. If it's blue, it's on. Remember that rule from now on because you'll be using it a lot.

Once your campaign launches, you'll have a better idea how each option functions. For now, I recommend using all four and using the suggested bids as simply suggestions. Suggested bids are not hard and fast. You don't need to spend money wastefully.

One way to mitigate any unnecessary spending comes down to using a super powerful feature in negative targeting. While newbies won't know what to place here, established advertisers use this option to refine their ad to target the right customers.

NEGATIVE KEYWORD & PRODUCT TARGETING

Boy, Amazon Advertising would be so simple if all we had to do was click a few boxes. However, for every ad you launch, you're starting from scratch, and Amazon treats each ad as brand new. This means that your ad will go out to everyone. Sure, it's great free advertising if no one ever clicks on your ad. On the flip side, lots of people will click on your ads, driving up your ad spend. To avoid that, use negative targeting.

Anyone new to Amazon Advertising won't know what to put here, and simply putting in guesses will only ruin your chances of success with that ad. If you are new, then leave this area blank. You'll fill it out as the campaign ages. More on that in the next chapter on analyzing your ads.

For now, let's dive in for a deeper understanding of why this section is fundamental to the success of your ad and future ads. When using **Negative Keyword Targeting**, you can insert a list of keywords you don't want your ad to appear on.

From our previous example, let's assume *The Home Exercise Plan* keeps being served to customers searching "home planning" and you aren't getting a single sale. Rather than allow Amazon to continue to plaster your ad on bad search queries, you can place the keyword term "home planning" in your negative targeting.

You'll have two choices for how you want that term suppressed. The first option is an *exact* match, meaning that anytime a customer types the *exact* keyword, then your ad will not show. When I place "home planning" as a negative exact match, customers who type "home planning" will never see my ad.

For the second option, negative phrase match, Amazon suppresses your ad when someone searches a deviation of the keyword. Let's say the customer types in "home planning for expectant parents." Though it's not exactly the keyword of "home planning" it's still within the phrase, therefore, Amazon will suppress your ad in search queries with that phrase match.

Pretty cool, right? I'd recommend leaving this section blank, again, if you do not have any data or experience with ads. It's best to leave it alone so you don't wonder why your ad isn't being served.

The next section is **Negative Product Targeting,** which focuses on products you do not want your ad served on. Unlike its counterpart, negative product targeting simply focuses on products and no deviations. Let's say you don't want your ad served on any competition. Simply insert the title or ASIN in the search box. Amazon will bring back all the choices related to your search. Click the Exclude link to put it on your list.

You'll find negative targeting handier once your ad has some traction and enough data to extrapolate for this option. Don't force it, and never assume some targeting won't work for your title. In the meantime, again, leave it blank if you have no data to support your selection.

CUSTOM TEXT AD

Though you learned this a little out of order, you'll most likely see this option if you choose the custom text ad feature. You'll get to see how your ad looks in a customer search. Take your time and do your best with copywriting. I highly recommend looking into Bryan Cohen's book *How to Write a Sizzling Synopsis* or Brian Meeks' *Mastering Amazon Ads* for the basics of copywriting. Otherwise, let's continue on.

I've found my conversion rate is much better on a standard ad with no custom text. I blame my tenuous grasp of copywriting. Rather than complicate the process, I stick to what I know—standard ads.

ALL SYSTEMS GO FOR AUTOMATIC TARGETING AD CAMPAIGNS

That's it! Either you can click the **Save as draft** button or **Launch campaign** button. Once you launch the campaign, Amazon will send you an email stating they received your ad request and will review it. The email will be something like this:

Subject line: Your "Keywords AUTO v1 071024" ad campaign is in review

Thank you for using Sponsored Products to advertise your products. Your ad "Keywords AUTO v1 071024" is currently under review by our moderators. The review process is usually completed within 24 hours but may take as long as 3 business days.

Don't worry about the moderated part. You're not in trouble, they're merely stating, "Hey, we got your ad request, and will give it a look ASAP."

Once they approve your ad, it sounds just as ominous as:

Subject line: Your "Keywords AUTO v1 071024" ad campaign has been moderated

Thank you for submitting your Sponsored Products ad campaign for review. Following an internal review, below is the status of your ads as per our Creative Acceptance Policies.

Below ads are eligible to be served on Amazon:

Your Ad, titled "Amazon Keywords for Books: How to Use Keywords for Better Discovery on Amazon (The Amazon Self Publisher Book 1)."

Don't worry, that's a positive message. I'm not sure who developed the canned response, but they need to amend it in a way that doesn't sound so foreboding. While the content of the email sounds safe, the subject line uses "moderated" in a way that seems like you did something wrong. Trust me, you're good. The main line you should focus on is *Below ads are eligible to be served on Amazon*—that's it.

You can visit your ads dashboard and see your automatic targeting ad working. You won't see any immediate results, and sometimes it'll take upwards of three days before you do. Just give it time and space to do its thing.

Should you find your ad is still not working after three days, you'll need a few strategies to figure out how to get it working. You'll learn more about that in a later chapter. For now, let's move on to the next level of advertising—manual targeting.

UNDERSTANDING MANUAL TARGETING FOR SPONSORED PRODUCT ADS

Manual targeting is by far my favorite option of all Amazon Advertising. With this ad type, you can refine your approach and reach a more targeted audience. Automatic targeting seems to spray and pray for the best results. Only when you use the negative targeting feature will an automatic targeted ad work better. With manual targeting, you're in complete control of where and how your ad shows.

The ad platform even states it best:

> "…*increase control over spend and bid more competitively.*"

I hope you've kept up with all the information up till now, because we're going to ramp up your understanding of more complex ads. A manual targeting ad starts exactly like the automatic campaign. Just select the Manual targeting option in the settings at the top.

When naming your campaign, try to include the type of manual targeting you plan to do, which can include:

1. Keywords
2. Products
3. Categories

Now, set your campaign bidding strategy, choose your ad format, and select the product you want to advertise. Then you have two choices:

1. Keyword targeting
2. Product targeting

Let's focus on these two unique paths, so you have a deeper understanding of your options. Not all ads are the same and you should treat each type differently in strategy and in setup.

KEYWORD TARGETING FOR MANUAL TARGETING ADS

For keyword targeting, Amazon serves your ads based on specific keywords customers search on their platform. You can have up to 1,000 keywords in one campaign, however, I urge you to not use that many. Your ad will struggle for any real relevancy with that many keyword targets. It might do well a time or two, but its shelf life is short. Why? Because it's hard for the algorithm to make sense of the huge and possibly strange mix of keyword terms.

Zero in on keywords you perceive are most relevant to your book. I avoid ambiguously relevant keywords because those terms could burn through my budget with no actual results. Can I get a customer to click on my ad on a loosely related keyword? Sure, but will that reader be my target audience? Probably not. Not all exposure is good exposure, so be selective with the terms that represent your book.

Getting the keywords right can be dicey because if you research this topic, you'll hear a ton of conflicting info. Rather than telling you any one method is better than the other, I recommend you try out what seems like the best fit.

The first way to find keywords for your manual targeting campaign is simply by running an automatic targeting ad. When running an auto-targeting ad, use the **Search Terms** report to gather data on what keywords performed best and what keywords wasted your budget. Use the best performing keywords (aka high performing keywords or HPKs) to start a manual targeting ad and set the bid according to the average CPC from the auto-targeting ad. Meanwhile, place the poor performing keywords from your auto-targeting ad into the negative keyword terms for the manual targeting campaign.

When you put a poor performing keyword into the negative targeting field, you're telling Amazon you don't want your ad served in front of that audience. Remember, you'll have two ways to use negative keywords—exact matches and phrase matches. When in doubt, use both options so you know that keyword won't eat up your budget again.

The next way to find keywords for your manual targeting campaign is through software like Publisher Rocket, KDSpy, Helium10, and more. All these options require an investment upfront or monthly subscriptions. My preferred software is Publisher Rocket (DaleLinks.com/Rocket) because it mines all the data I need to run a successful ads campaign. I don't use all the keywords given to me. I simply cherry-pick the options and use what I perceive as relevant. Some advertisers never question Publisher Rocket and just use the data given for a campaign, but I'm not that way. Maybe it's my type-A personality, but I like to lose my money because *I* messed up, *not* software.

If you're lacking cash, you can always find your keywords the old-fashioned way—the Amazon search bar. First, you'll need to open your browser in incognito mode so you don't taint the results with keywords customized to you. Whenever you visit Amazon, they track you, your browsing history, and your buying patterns. Then, when you use Amazon's search engine, they'll customize the keyword autosuggestions based on the customer data they've collected. You need to avoid that, so that's why we go to an incognito browser to remove any personal identifying information. You'll then get keywords based on the vast majority of browsing customers.

Go to Amazon.com and visit the Kindle Store or Books in the category drop-down of the search bar. Now, type in any related root keyword. For instance, if your book is a car repair manual, start typing "car," then stop. Let Amazon recommend keywords for you. Remember, keywords are not just a single word, but more accurately a string of words grouped together in a phrase.

What does the autosuggestion give you? Jot down all the options you see as relevant to your title. Once you note all your options, type another letter or word after "car." You'll find many new keyword options. Simply rinse and repeat. Once you think you're done, use the ABC search option. Type your root keyword then the letter "a." Note all your choices. Then, remove the "a" and type the letter "b." Cycle through the whole alphabet to exhaust all your options. Leave no stone unturned.

How long will this take? As long as you want it to. As a rough example, if you're looking to generate about 1,000 keywords, this process can take several hours. I lean in favor of running an automatic targeting ad which gives me good choices. Or I use Publisher Rocket and finish my targeting research in seconds.

The good news is if you're using the old-fashioned way of mining keywords, you won't have to do it too often. You can use that set of keywords on many campaigns to come and even see how well they pay off. The best practice is to keep all your keywords on a spreadsheet so when you find an HPK or a poor converting keyword, you have that data ready for any new ads you launch. As your ads mature, you'll get even more data. It's the circle of life; you'll use one ad to start another and so on.

> *Fun fact: Amazon Advertising recommends using keywords with misspellings. Since customers don't always search with the correct spelling, you might as well meet them where they are.*

The last way of finding keywords is directly through the ad setup. Admittedly, these are not the best keywords and often have very little perceived relevance. In the **Keyword targeting** section, Amazon will suggest keywords based on your book's metadata and related products within your niche. Sometimes, you'll see 100 keywords or fewer. That's actually quite good!

Let's talk about strategy now that you have the keywords. Rather than packing your ad with keywords, go light. In fact, 100 keywords are probably more than sufficient for a new ad. As the ad matures, you can add, pause, or negatively categorize keywords as you see fit.

The more you fine-tune your ad, the better it will be at spending less while earning more. That's the key, right?

If you want to enter your own keywords, you can copy and paste them into the **Enter list** tab or upload a spreadsheet to the **Upload File** tab. When you select your keywords, you'll have a choice of **Suggested bid**, **Custom bid**, and **Default bid**. The latter two options allow you to set the bids while suggested relies on Amazon for the bids that work best for the keyword. I typically select default bid so any keywords added to this campaign will come in at the default amount I want. You can always go back later and change the individual keyword bidding based on your results.

KEYWORD MATCH TYPES

Now comes the part that gets even trickier. You must choose between three keyword match types, including:

1. Broad
2. Phrase
3. Exact

Can you choose all three for a single campaign? Sure, but I wouldn't recommend it. The point is to build effective ad campaigns you can evaluate efficiently. I suggest creating different ad sets based on each of the three keyword matches because all three function differently, especially when it comes to the bidding strategy.

The broad match keyword is a loosely related set of words related to your targeted keyword. For example, if your keyword is "home exercises," the customer's search term might be "exercising at home for seniors." There's overlap between the terms, and they share a common denominator in some fashion, so these are possible connections the algorithm will make if you run an ad with broad keyword matches. Another example would be "bicycle helmet" and the customer searches "cycling accessories."

Phrase match keywords are a bit more dialed in and have some precision. Where broad matches are loosely related keywords, phrase matches include a root keyword with some deviation. For instance, my keyword might be "shapeshifter romance." If the customer types in "werebear shapeshifter romance novel," the root keyword is in it, but it also reaches beyond the root keyword with other identifying words. When you're using a phrase match, you're telling Amazon you specifically want customers to say what you're saying, but you welcome additional words in the original keyword phrase.

The last match type is an exact. I'm sure you know what it means based on the word "exact." Whatever keyword you choose, the customer must search for exactly. With an exact match, you're telling Amazon you want a specific customer search and nothing else. No deviations. No misspellings. Nothing but what you asked for. The only exception is pluralization. If you select "bats" and the exact match was "bat," those are considered the same thing.

Exact matches are great for focusing on your ideal customer. If you are certain your audience searches for a specific keyword term, then go with the exact match. There is a small catch, though, in how much a keyword costs based on the match type.

Can you bid the same for all match types? Sure, but will it work? Possibly not, because the narrower your focus becomes, the more expensive it is to reach the customer. Broad keywords cost the least since you're casting a wider net. You might catch a few good keywords in a broad match, but a large portion might not work for you since you're relying on customers to type the right term based on your book while still having interest in your niche.

For phrase matches, you'll want to spend about 20% to 25% more on your CPC[x] than your broad match. Though your audience isn't nearly as narrow as they will be with an exact phrase match, you'll still pay a bit more for winning a bid.

Exact matches cost about 25% to 35% more than phrase match keywords.[xi] Because you're asking to find a super specific audience, you'll need to pay a bit more. The nice part is you're drilling down so deep that your chances of conversion should drastically increase.

In terms of the hierarchy of match types, the basic match is broad, the specific match is phrase, and the precision match is exact. The more refined your search requirements, the more it's going to cost. The gamble can pay off with just the right keyword for your book.

SETTING THE MATCH TYPE & BID

When you come to the keyword targeting section, upload or select your keywords and set one match type. Save those same keywords for another two campaigns where you can break out into each match type. Those lacking the budget should stick with running broad matches on their first ad. As the budget improves and earnings grow, then build out the other campaign types, scaling toward the most expensive match type in exact.

Once you know your match type, simply click **Add keywords** and they'll all move over into the campaign keywords column on the right. Scroll through the keywords and sift out any undesirable or less relevant keywords. If it's ready, then let's move on!

The next section is negative keyword targeting. If you ran any previous campaigns and have a list of your poor performing keywords, enter them here. You'll have two choices: **Negative exact** and **Negative Phrase**. Your ad will not show when customers search for these keywords. Again, with negative keywords, you don't have to pay a dime. These are there to help your ad perform better in the long run.

Those of you just running your first ad should simply leave this blank. Remember, no guessing allowed in this area. It's the difference between an effective ad and a broken ad.

Once you're set, you're ready to click the **Launch campaign** button in the bottom right. Much like the other ads, you'll get a confirmation email followed by an approval or rejection email. It usually takes less than a day for the ads platform to vet your ad.

> *Fun fact: Did you know the algorithm ignores some words like "the," "of," "when," "if," and "and." They're considered somewhat useless to the algorithm.*

PRODUCT TARGETING WITH CATEGORIES FOR MANUAL TARGETING ADS

Assuming you aren't using keyword targeting, you can select product targeting, which covers specific products and categories. These ads will show on product pages, in categories, and in search result pages. Each product targeting type carries different roles.

For categories, Amazon serves your ad to books and products relevant to your niche or browse path. On Amazon, the platform creates a trail of breadcrumbs, starting with the main category and drilling down into a more niche topic. For example, my collection of short stories would probably fit into the browse path of:

Books – Literature & Fiction – Short Stories & Anthologies – Short Stories Anthologies

Books is the general category which narrows down to the category of Literature & Fiction. The browse path doesn't simply end there but branches out into various other niches. I chose Short Stories & Anthologies. Beyond that category, I go deeper into the subniche of Short Stories Anthologies. My book is one of many options in its category.

Think of browse paths as a distant cousin to the Dewey Decimal system at the library. Amazon categorizes products into subcategories for a better browsing experience for their customers. While you may not find the previously mentioned browse path at a local library, it is on Amazon's platform. I'm sure you know that Amazon's categorization system is 100% proprietary. Amazon is continually adding and subtracting categories based on customer demand.

Understanding the function of categories (aka browse paths), you're given the choice to serve your ad in a category that can include tens of thousands of other books. For instance, in the previous browse path, there are 12,242 to 20,403 products. The nice thing is Amazon makes that data available in your dashboard based on the **Suggested** tab in the **Product targeting** section. Amazon determines this suggestion based on your book's metadata and current category selection.

Should you want to find better options, go to the **Search** tab next to **Suggested**. Type in words related to your niche and see what

Amazon brings back. Keep your category selections limited between one and three. A single category has a lot of opportunity to advertise, therefore, if you select a ton of categories, you're going to get served out to way more categories than your ad can handle. This type of reach is good but can work against you if you aren't careful. After all, your ad may not be relevant to all the targets for each category, leading you to spending more than you'd like.

Once you find the category you want, you'll need to set your bidding. In the bid drop-down menu, you'll have familiar choices in suggested, custom and default. Much like previous ads, set the CPC according to what works best for your title.

Having one to three categories selected, you can now move onto the **Negative Product Targeting** section. As mentioned previously, leave this area blank if you don't have data from previous campaigns. You can later add products or brands to negative targeting that aren't converting well in this ad or other ads.

Once you're set, either select the **Save as draft** button or **Launch campaign** button. When you save as a draft, you can always come back to your ads dashboard and find the ad under the **Draft** tab. You know by now that once you launch the campaign, you'll get an email confirmation followed by the "moderated" email confirmation.

Using categories in your **Product Targeting** ads is like **Automatic Targeting** ads. Amazon does all the footwork for you, so all you have to do is analyze the data, adjust your campaign, and scale with what you know. Category ads appear in front of thousands of products at a time, and while not all products will prove worthy, knowing what does and doesn't convert will help you with the current and future ad campaigns.

Assuming you already know the best products for converting sales, you can skip the **Categories** tab in the Product targeting section and choose **Individual products**.

TARGETING WITH INDIVIDUAL PRODUCTS FOR MANUAL TARGETING ADS

The entire campaign setup works the same as category ads—settings, campaign bidding strategy, ad format, create an ad group, and your books—but now we select the **Individual products** tab in the **Product targeting** section. You have three ways to add products to your campaign:

1. **Suggested.** As you'd guess, Amazon recommends books similar to yours.
2. **Search.** When in doubt, search it out. The search bar works exactly like the one on Amazon's marketplace.
3. **Enter list.** If you already have a list of products from previous campaigns or through other means, upload it here. The ASIN (Amazon Standard Identification Number) is all you need for this section, so avoid using titles or author names.

Adjust your bid in the drop-down with suggested, custom, or default. Suggested is what Amazon recommends based on other advertisers' bids. For custom, you can set it to your liking. Default is the starting bid you set on the campaign. Once you see a product you like, click the **Add** link next to the product and you're done. If you enter the wrong product, you can always remove it from the campaign by clicking the **Remove all** function or the **X** function next to the product.

Once you're done, either save it as a draft or launch the campaign. Then, monitor the ad's performance after it launches. You'll love how well product ads convert if you pay close attention to them. It's been my experience that the CPCs are higher, like exact keyword matches. Since you're going granular on who your ad serves to, Amazon charges a bit more.

SETTING UP A SPONSORED BRAND AD

Sponsored Brand Ads are the next step up from the Product Ads. While I'm all-in with Sponsored Product Ads, I stress caution with brand ads. They cost a bit more since they receive prime placement in the Amazon search results. When using the brand ads, you get a banner of three or more of your books displayed on search pages. Since it's at the very top, quite a few people will click on the ad unintentionally, selecting something that may or may not resonate with them.

Once a customer clicks on your banner ad, they'll be sent to a landing page with all your advertised books. They'll see all the books and one hero product, typically your first selected book, displayed in the middle of the site. You won't have to worry about setting up this landing page since Amazon Advertising automates the whole thing for you.

Go through the normal ad setup, but this time, select the Sponsored Brands feature. Under the **Settings** section, name your campaign, select a portfolio, set your start and end dates, and then focus on your budget.

Unlike **Sponsored Product** ads, you can set your budget for **Daily** or **Lifetime**. Let's say you only have $300 to put towards ads, then select **Lifetime** budget. This gives your ad a specific amount to spend before it ends. Whichever comes first, Lifetime budget or the end date, is when Amazon stops the ad.

I lean in favor of daily budget since I bid a little lower. When bidding low, you can expect crickets at first, but you don't burn through as much of your budget. Then, as the ad matures and gets some experience, I typically increase the CPC based on the targeting.

In the next section, **Author**, you'll select the name associated with the brand you're advertising. Don't skip this part since Amazon organizes the next section, **Products**, based on your author choice. When you scroll down, you'll see all the titles associated with the author name. Unlike the previous ad types, you must select at least three books while Amazon recommends up to five or more. Having a couple extra titles in the ad helps keep the ad running should a title be out of stock.

Now that you have the books selected, you can preview the landing page. Choose **Preview your landing page** just below your books. Scroll a little farther down and you'll see the ad preview on the right side. The display will show how the ad will look on mobile and desktop.

On the left side under Creative, upload an appropriate author profile picture. A square image that isn't too large works best. Simply select **Edit picture**, find your author picture on your computer, then upload it there. You'll see your ad update with the new picture.

Even though you can select five titles or more, Amazon will only display three of the titles on the banner ad. Organize your selections based on what you feel looks best or fits the proper order in a series.

Drag and drop the order you want the books to appear. If you don't want one of the three products displayed on the banner, click **Change Product** to be given a different choice from the books advertised on the main landing page.

Next up is the **Headline** box. Come up with a catchy headline that'll command attention and get the customers clicking on your ad. You can have up to fifty characters, so use that space wisely. The same rules apply to the headline as custom text in previous ads. Stay away from unsubstantiated claims, special sales, and all caps. Otherwise, you should be good.

TARGETING FOR SPONSORED BRAND ADS

Since you already know how to set up Sponsored Product Ads, this next section should be a breeze. Whether you're selecting keyword or product targeting, the same principles apply here. Take your time and always separate your ad types to avoid confusion when glancing at your ads dashboard. You need to assess your ads quickly. Keeping the ad types separated cuts down on time spent analyzing.

In fact, I separate ads into separate portfolios based on the product and ad type. Then, if the ads get messy, I can easily pop into each portfolio and quickly evaluate how well an ad is performing.

Choosing your negative targeting works the same as before. Simply wait to get the right data before suppressing specific keywords and products. Never jump the gun and assume a target isn't worth pursuing. The only exception to this rule is if you are vehemently against serving your ad in front of a competitor. Even then, I wouldn't recommend skipping on competitors since they have a built-in audience who may find your content appealing.

SETTING UP A LOCKSCREEN AD

I'm not a fan of **Lockscreen Ads**. This ad type serves customers based on broad interest sets. The ads appear on Amazon-powered e-readers and tablets before the customer can access their main screen or at the bottom of the Kindle after opening. Despite my reservations about **Lockscreen Ads**, you should still have a basic overview of how to set these up so you can make your own informed decision on this ad type.

The other major sticking point with **Lockscreen Ads** is they are only available on Amazon.com. Why haven't other regions rolled out this ad type? Amazon Advertising has offered this option for quite a few years in the U.S. with no signs of expanding into other regions. Ultimately, I can only speculate on why they don't have it elsewhere. For now, I stress caution when breaking into **Lockscreen Ads**.

In the **Settings** section, you'll notice a substantial difference in the setup. Sure, you can name your campaign like usual. When you get to the start and end date, you'll notice you cannot run an open-ended campaign with no expiration. This is because you set a lifetime budget for the ad. The minimum budget to start is $100 or more, which can be off-putting if you never set up a lockscreen ad before.

The lifetime budget spend applies to the entire campaign. Running a campaign that lasts ninety days may only use a budget of $1 or so a day. Of course, this is all predicated on the pacing you select. When you run your campaign as quickly as possible, Amazon won't mess around and will serve your ad out right away. If you're not looking to blow your budget all in one day, select the spread campaign evenly over its duration. The latter option is what I use and saw the best results.

For an evenly spread campaign, if you're under budget, Amazon rolls the excess budget over to the subsequent days. This means if you spend very little at first, your ad will use the budget later in the life cycle.

> *Fair warning: Once you set pacing on a lockscreen ad, you cannot change it. You can always change the end date or increase your budget, but you cannot change the pacing.*

As per usual, select the one book you want to advertise and move onto the **Interest targeting** section. This option is probably the most problematic of the whole ad setup. It's not very intuitive and you'll have to stumble your way through their categories. No search feature. No recommendations. Nothing to make you feel you're selecting the right category.

To make matters worse, the categories they display are not the same categories you see on their website. The selection is essentially like the BISAC (Book Industry Standards and Communications) codes KDP used to use in the publishing process.

You can forget about going granular or hyper-focusing your targets. The only way to find out if a category works is by launching one of these campaigns and testing out your options. This is largely why readers get ads that aren't really aligned with their interests on their lockscreen display.

While bidding is rather complex in the previous ad types, Amazon keeps it dead simple for lockscreen ads. In their words:

> *The budget must be at least 100x your bid. Example: With a budget of $100.00, your bid can't exceed $1.00.*

If you want to bid anywhere above $1 per click but budgeted $100, forget about it. Amazon won't allow it. Then again, you won't find too many times when you want to bid that high anyway, especially for ebooks or print books with lower pricing.

In the **Creative** section, you're going to dial in your ad copy to entice browsing customers into buying. Much like the Sponsored Product Ads Custom Text feature, you only have 150 characters to get it right. Just below the custom text box, you'll see how your ad will appear on Kindle devices and the Fire Tablet. If you're happy with the selection, hit the **Launch campaign** button to get things going.

ANALYZING THE DATA TO OPTIMIZE THE AD

Setting up ads is a cinch, regardless of what you choose. However, the work has only just begun. You're going to need to dive deeper into your analytics to make informed decisions and build profitable ad campaigns. Take your time understanding the setup, because once you know what you're looking for, analyzing the data comes easier. However, analyzing your ads can be time-consuming.

Since you've already set up your ads based on my recommendations, viewing the results should be more efficient. I suggested naming your campaigns specifically and organizing those campaigns into portfolios. The less time you spend messing with your ads dashboard, the more time you have for other things, like writing your next book or marketing in other avenues.

Before diving deeper into the analytics, let's organize your dashboard according to what we need to see at a glance. Under the main dashboard area, also known as the **Management** tab, you'll see a giant graph. Once your ads serve, you'll see two lines: spend and sales. If you want to add more items to this graphic, simply click the **+Add** metric button on the far right. Add the impressions, clicks, and ACoS (advertising cost of sale). You can display up to five metrics above the graph.

ANALYZING THE DATA TO OPTIMIZE THE AD

Below the graph, you'll see your ads separated into rows and columns which display the metrics from your campaign. Select the **Columns** drop-down feature at the top right corner above the ads. Now, pick **Customize columns** and a window will pop up. Keep in mind that you can change what displays in the columns, whether on an account or campaign level. The more experience you have with Amazon ads, the more you can dial in these columns to suit your needs. For now, I'll give you my recommended settings.

In the pop-up menu, deselect all elements and choose these items:

- Budget
- Impressions
- Clicks
- Spend
- Cost-per-click (CPC)
- Orders
- Sales
- Advertising cost of sales (ACoS)
- Optional: KENP read (Kindle edition normalized page count) and Estimated KENP royalties. These metrics only pertain to KDP Select-enrolled ebooks.

These elements are going to give you a quick snapshot of how an ad is performing. While Amazon continues to improve their dashboard with new metrics and features, the previously mentioned options are ideal for a quick glance. With these analytics, you can make a quick judgement on how to best move forward in a campaign.

While many Amazon Advertising experts will tell you focusing on any one element is a recipe for disappointment, I have to disagree.

If you want to save time, then quickly focusing on these elements will tell you how well a campaign performs. It's not until these numbers look a little off or the ad spend goes above your liking that you need to dive deeper.

AT A GLANCE STATS

When running your first ad campaign, you may not have much movement, especially if your ad spend and cost-per-click is low. Don't stress about it because this process will take time. You may find your ad takes off if you already have a book with consistently high sales. In the meantime, you'll need to consider a few things.

When first logging into the Amazon Advertising dashboard, take a quick glance at the numbers. All you need is a bird's eye view of how your ads are performing. You won't need to dive deep into each ad and the targeting until you have a substantial number of impressions and clicks. Naturally, sales would be ideal. As long as you're getting some movement on your ad, you have data to analyze.

Focus on impressions, clicks, and ACoS. While these metrics only give you a glimpse of how your ads perform, it's all you'll need at first. Don't rely on these three metrics alone as your ad ages. You'll need other metrics like the ones previously mentioned. Also, you'll soon learn a method for cross-checking the effectiveness of your ad. For now, let's look at the three at-a-glance stats so you can be efficient in your dashboard.

If you're getting impressions, you're bidding the right amount for placement on Amazon. Does that mean you have first position placement? No, it merely shows that Amazon is serving your ad. If you're getting no impressions, then chances are likely you're bidding too low on a given target. You'll notice for some targets you'll get a ton of impressions at a set bid while others get nothing.

Why is that? Relevancy!

This is why I had you learn the "why" before you learned the "how" of Amazon Advertising.

When your book carries lower relevancy, Amazon has less confidence serving your ad to customers. Whereas books with a proven track record tend to win the best placements for ads.

Does this mean you don't stand a chance against your competition?

Not necessarily. In fact, you still have a pretty good chance. It has a lot to do with timing. You're competing against lots of other advertisers. Some have books with more relevancy, while others carry very little relevance. The good news is that even though Amazon favors the products with the most relevancy, there are still tons of placements for ads across the platform. Don't lose heart; there's still hope.

You're only one good ad away from building more relevancy and getting better ad placement. Running ads will feel like rolling a boulder uphill. As long as you don't give up, you'll eventually hit your stride and the boulder will roll downhill, making everything much easier for you.

For targeting that has impressions within the first few days, leave the bidding as is. Simply increasing the bid will not increase your chances of serving to more people. Let it ride to see how it plays out.

If you're not getting impressions on a target, you'll need to increase your bidding. Wait at least two to three days before increasing the

CPC a little. For instance, if your bidding was $0.35, then increase it to $0.36 or $0.37. Step back and let it sit for another few days before increasing. Just don't increase the bid above a realistic break-even point.

As mentioned previously, placing a bid higher than $1 places you in a compromising position. Unproven targeting with a higher bid is risky. Where you have a lower bid, you can afford to have a lower conversion rate. Once you get to a higher bid, your conversion rate better be rock solid. Your profits should be a gauge of your break-even point.

Assuming my profit margin is $3 per book and I set my bid at $1, then I better convert, as a minimum, one out of every three clicks. Yikes! And that's just to break even. While one sale helps with building relevancy, it's not enough to make any major impact with the algorithm. Realistically, you'll need to get hundreds of sales in a given day before you see a bump in algorithmic relevance.

Once you hit your maximum bidding threshold for breaking even, cut your losses and pause the targeting. It's not that you shouldn't use that targeting; instead, it's likely it's not working for this ad right now. No need to add the targeting to your negative targeting since it really hasn't proved itself. Try the targeting on another campaign later.

It's super important you prune your ads a bit. You should pause any weak performing targets so you don't degrade the effectiveness of your ad campaign. The more targeted your ad is, the more it'll benefit you. You *can* have targeting that doesn't bring in impressions. You may want to consider removing it eventually if you're getting no results.

Assuming you're doing fine with impressions, then we have to focus on the next metric—clicks. Are customers actually clicking on your ad? Without clicks, you won't spend a dime on an ad. With clicks, you'll see some results. Will the results be good? That remains to be seen since not all clicks are created equal.

You'll want to see about 1,000 impressions to 1 click. That's a best-case scenario at first. If you see that ratio, then you know things should be good. Double check your ad spend to make sure it's not through the roof. If you're under budget every day, then you're probably ready. Simply go into your ad, prune any dead targeting, or increase the bid.

The next metric I focus on at a glance is the ACoS. Amazon describes the advertising cost of sale like this:

> *The percentage of your sales that you spend on advertising. This is calculated by dividing your spend by sales attributed to your ads. Attribution varies by campaign type.*

With targeting that gets impressions and clicks but no sales, you'll see a big fat goose egg (0%). That's not good, because it shows you're spending money while getting no sales. Whereas when you see an increase in the ACoS percentage, it can be good *or* bad.

While this isn't the method you should use for deeply analyzing your ad, it's effective for making a quick judgment on how your ads are performing. Don't use this method if your ACoS goes above a certain percentage.

Each sale of your book is going to provide you a set royalty. For ebooks, it's 35% or 70% based on what you selected in your KDP dashboard upon publishing. For print books, it gets dicey since Amazon pays 60% minus print fees. That means you aren't really getting paid the full 60%.

Let's do the math in this example. My book *The Amazon Self Publisher* sells for $24.99. Print fees are $4.71 and my royalty per sale is $10.28. Wait…that's less than half the retail cost.

What happened? Those damned print fees eat up our bottom line, especially if your book has a lot of pages like mine does. For every page printed beyond 108 pages, Amazon deducts about $0.01 to $0.03 per page.

Based on the retail price and print fees, let's figure out the net royalty. You'll want to take your total profit and divide it by the retail price to get your percentage. Keep in mind, the number will come out as fractional. Simply move the decimal point over two numbers to the right. Use only the first two numbers and don't worry about rounding up or down. For my book, here's how the equation would look:

$$\$10.28 \div \$24.99 = 0.41$$

$$0.41 = 41\%$$

The royalty for that print book is roughly 41%. This is going to play a huge role in our quick glance at stats, especially involving the ACoS percentage.

This is where I have to stress:

THIS IS NOT A METHOD FOR ALWAYS TRACKING YOUR ADS.

It's simply a way of quickly judging how the ad is performing overall. Remember, Amazon states that the ads dashboard can take upwards of 72 hours to update. That's why it's important to look at the entire picture and not just the ACoS.

To see how well your targeting or overall ad is performing, take your royalty and subtract the ACoS displayed. The remaining amount is your net profit.

For *The Amazon Self Publisher*, I have an ad running that has an ACoS of 13.5%. I can already see at a glance the ad is performing above the break-even point and I'm profiting about 27.5% per sale. The math would look like this:

41% (royalty) - 13.5% (ACoS) = 27.5% net profit

It's safe to say I made about $6.87 after subtracting ad spend from my royalty. Here's how I worked it out:

$24.99 (retail) x 27.5% = $6.87

The big issue is the brand halo effect, where a customer clicks an ad yet doesn't buy the product advertised. Should the customer buy another book related to the advertised book, Amazon shows credit. While this sounds great, it can be an issue when you consider ebook and print book royalties. When you check the sales of an ebook ad, but see a different price, it can be confusing.

Why? Because the brand halo effect occurs when Amazon takes credit for converting the sale of a book in your brand. While getting a sale is better than nothing at all, it's going to mess up your stats at a glance.

Now, we have to account for what type of sales occur on an ad. Usually, you can make an educated guess, but once an ad campaign takes off, it becomes harder to know the proper attribution of an ebook or a print book sale.

To make it easier, I recommend using the lower royalty to calculate your stats at a glance. For instance, if I sell my ebook at $9.99 with a 70% royalty and my paperback is $24.99 with a 41% royalty, I'll use the lower of the two for determining if this ad is at or below a break-even point.

If the ad's ACoS is at or below 41%, then we're gold. I'll get my ad above 0% but below 26% which is 15% less than the break-even point. I like to account for any delays in clicks or sales on the ad, so 15% seems more than sufficient.

This method of quickly glancing at your stats will save you on days where you have little to no time for fussing with ads. While I encourage checking your ads daily, it's sometimes not practical considering all the things you have to do as an author.

Should the ACoS stay at 0% or above the break-even point, you'll have to take the time to look over the ad and figure out what's holding it back or draining your budget.

What do you look for when analyzing and adjusting an ad? How do you keep an ad performing well? Let's look under the hood.

ANALYZING YOUR TARGETING

Go to an ad you want to analyze, click on the campaign name, then the ad group where applicable. You should now see the products advertised in this ad. On the left sidebar, select the **Targeting** option to see how your ad is doing on each target.

As a reminder, if you haven't done so already, customize your columns to include:

1. Impressions
2. Clicks
3. Spend
4. Cost-per-click (CPC)
5. Orders
6. Sales
7. ACoS
8. Optional: KENP Read. This is only for books enrolled in the KDP Select program. If you don't have an ebook in the KDP Select Program, then skip this. If the ebook advertised isn't in KDP Select and you have another ebook in the program, use this column. Due to brand halo effect, a browsing customer could find another title in your backlog that's available in Kindle Unlimited and check it out. Your ad will display the pages read if that's the case.
9. Optional: Suggested bid. This isn't essential but can give you clues if your targeting isn't getting any impressions.

For automatic targeting ads, you'll see the four groups in substitutes, loose match, complements, and close match. For manual targeting ads, you'll notice the individual targets such as the keywords, products, and categories. Look across each column and you'll see the need-to-know information.

Let's look at the number of impressions a target is producing. Should you find no impressions after running the ad a few days, slightly increase your bid. Conversely, targeting with lots of impressions means you're bidding the right amount to serve on Amazon. I recommend clicking the top of the column of impressions once to organize from least to most. When you click the column again, you'll see most to least.

I like to see what isn't performing and adjust accordingly. Let's start with sorting from least to most. Assuming your campaign has over 50 targets, adjust the results per page to the maximum of 300. You'll find a drop-down menu in the bottom right of the ad. Once you have all your targeting organized from least to most, look for the targets with no impressions after a few days.

You can always increase the bid slightly here. In the event you find the targeting might not bear much relevance to your ad, tick the switch to the left of the targeting to pause it. Don't worry, you are not pausing your ad. You're simply removing the option that isn't performing, allowing Amazon to serve your ad in other areas where it may work better. Try bidding higher if your budget allows for it before pausing the target. You never know if that might kickstart that target.

If you enabled the **Suggested bid** column, you'll notice a recommended bid, and a suggested range for bidding based on what other advertisers are currently bidding for placement. Again, even though it might be high, that doesn't mean you should follow suit. Sure, you can bid high and possibly win placement for that target, but at what cost? Be selective about how high you bid on a target.

Meanwhile, don't be afraid to stand your ground on a target's bid if you're getting impressions. Should those impressions slow down, try increasing the bid.

Now, let's consider the targets getting the highest numbers of impressions. Sort the column by clicking on it once. To be clear, just because a target has a ton of impressions doesn't mean it's worth holding onto. That's why you need to look at clicks next. How many impressions does it take before you get a click? You can figure out the conversion by dividing the number of impressions by the clicks.

For example, I have a category target with 21,174 impressions and 11 clicks. Here's how the math works out:

$$21{,}174 \div 11 = 1{,}924$$

Based on this example, I'm converting 1 click out of every 1,924 impressions. It's not bad, but it's not great. Does it work against us? At that level, possibly not. At least I'm getting clicks, therefore increasing relevancy for the ad, but that metric alone won't be as effective as converting a sale. Remember, Amazon loves conversions, so if your ad converts browsing customers into buyers, you're made!

Before moving on, look at how much you spent in the **Spend** column and your average CPC. These columns tell you how much you're paying for the target and for each customer click. Avoid any knee-jerk reactions when looking at the **Spend** column. If you look at the sales, you'll get the best picture.

If your sales figure is higher than your spend, that doesn't necessarily indicate a "good" result. Remember, Amazon credits your account with the retail cost of the item, hence why I recommend checking your ACoS when glancing at your ad. Then, you can truly figure out if your ad is performing as you want.

When the ACoS is at or above your royalty, don't sweat it. You simply have to do some deeper investigation. While it takes up to 72 hours for Amazon to report the data for sales, you can always cross-check the number of sales you got in the period.

It's always a good idea before running an ad to establish a baseline of sales. Go with the average number of sales per month. If you're getting 50 sales per month, then see 75 sales per month when the ad runs, you can theorize the ads are working. If your average is 50 sales and you see a drop, then the ad isn't working its magic and you'll need to consider pruning any targets draining your budget.

Amazon recommends you drop your bid on low-performing targets. Some targets take a bit to warm up, therefore making it tough to extrapolate anything from a handful of impressions and clicks. Rather than having the targeting burn through your budget, simply lower your CPC. Should impressions drop significantly, kick the bid up again or pause the target just to be safe.

Do you want to add the poor performing target to your negative targeting? No, not just yet. We need a better idea of what's going on. Sometimes, a target might not convert a sale based on the type. For instance, you could have a keyword target as a broad match that doesn't convert well. It may not be the keyword itself, but the variations customers type into the search bar. You'll learn how to find out how the keyword isn't benefiting you and the way to suppress deviations of the poor performing broad match keywords.

As your ad matures, you'll separate the wheat from the chaff and find out what is working for or against your ad campaign. When in doubt, pause a poor performing target. The worst thing that could happen is you save some money, and the ad campaign loses momentum. No big deal. Simply start a new ad group with the information you got from the first ad group.

> Digital clutter will eat away at your sanity. When pausing words or campaigns, you'll see a mixture of paused and active targets and campaigns. If you're done with the paused item, you can easily hide it from view and bring it back up when you need it later.
>
> Simply click the **Filter by** drop-down menu and select the **Active status** option. Two drop-down menus appear above the columns with **Active status** and **All**. Select the **All** drop-down menu and click the **Enabled** option. Now, click the **Apply** button to clear out all the paused targets and ads.
>
> Presto! All your pesky paused items disappear. If having paused ads interferes with your workflow, you can always archive them. Tick the box next to the ad or target, then click the **Archive** button just above the columns.

When you have hundreds of targets on an ad, it'll take more time to adjust each one individually. Therefore, sorting makes your life easier. Once you find the targets you want to adjust—whether through bids, archiving or pausing—you can tick the box next to the target and the menu of options above the columns include:

- **Adjust bid**—this quick and easy option applies a set bid across multiple targets
- **Apply adjusted bid**—if the suggested bid makes sense and doesn't kill your budget, this option is for you

- **Pause**
- **Archive**

Choose wisely when applying any of those options. It can get really messy if you aren't careful with what you select. Accidentally archiving or pausing high performing targets can be counterproductive.

Once you kick around in your ads dashboard over the first few weeks, you'll get used to these features and become more familiar with any additional features Amazon rolls out. Take your time, explore and, when in doubt, contact support to show you the ins and outs of your ads dashboard.

It doesn't stop here, because now you'll refine your ads with the best feature in your dashboard – **Search Term** reports. That's your guide to how an ad performs and gives you a peek behind the curtain to see what's really working in your campaigns.

SEARCH TERMS REPORT: THE CHEAT SHEET TO BUILDING BETTER ADS

In 2017, I dove into Amazon Advertising, simply guessing my way through it. I wasn't too sure about what customers searched to see my ad or the exact keyword a customer used when buying my book through an ad. That all changed when Amazon introduced the **Search Terms** report.

The search terms report gives you all the history of the ad from the past 65 days or fewer. For whatever reason, Amazon doesn't allow for lifetime viewing, so you'll need to check and back up these reports at least once per month. To back up your search terms report, narrow down to the time frame you want in the **Date range** box in the top right above the columns. Then, select the **Export** button to get a spreadsheet of all the data. You'll end up using this report to build out new campaigns and refine current campaigns.

I highly recommend setting up an automated download of your Search Terms report every month. Select the Measurements & Reporting option on the left side menu. Click the Create report button, then fill in all the criteria. Once you're set, click the Run report button in the top right. Then, once a month, you'll get an email notification from Amazon Ads that your report is ready for download. If you miss the notification, you can always come back into this section and download the report for each specific advertising period.

On the ad level, you'll see an option in the left sidebar labeled **Search Terms**. Select that option to see what customers search or land on when discovering your ad.

For keyword targeting, you'll see what the customer typed in the search bar to get your ad. This reveals clues about how your potential audience views your book as it relates to their search term. First, organize according to what performs best.

Tap the top of the **Clicks** column to organize most to least. If you're getting a lot of clicks with no buys, then consider pausing or even suppressing the target. Tick the box next to the poor performing target. You'll get two options: **Add as keyword** or **Add as negative keyword**. Choose the latter option to suppress that keyword for this ad. A pop-up menu appears giving you two options in a drop-down menu: **Negative exact** and **Negative phrase**. Choose exact so anyone searching that exact keyword will not see your ad. For negative phrase, you'll use the exact match with a slight deviation in the keyword.

If you want to add the keyword to both exact and phrase, you may have to add it manually to your **Negative targeting** tab in the left sidebar. Amazon seems to be ironing out some features and, for whatever reason, only allows you to add a target to one option or the other.

For category or product targeting, you'll see the matched product and the product targets (or categories). Again, sort the columns based on what is performing least and sift out those targets if they're draining your budget or have no relevance to your ad. Unlike keywords in the **Search Terms** section, you have only one negative targeting option. Once you add it to the negative targeting, you're set.

In the event you see a target performing particularly well, you'll want to double down on that target. If the target isn't already in your campaign, simply tick the box next to the targeting and add it to your ad group's targeting. You'll have to set the bid before Amazon allows you to add it. Look at the CPC for the target and bid accordingly.

The longer you run your ad, the more you can tweak the settings and increase the likelihood of better conversions. Focus on the targets that convert sales while suppressing targets with no sales that drain your budget. At first, it's going to seem like an uphill battle, but the more you work with ads, the easier it gets.

As you build out your ads, save all targets that perform best for a given title. Store them all in a spreadsheet so you can build future campaigns based on these high performing keywords (aka HPKs). Likewise, when you see repeat offenders in negative targeting, build a spreadsheet with those targets. Of course, you'll want to have separate spreadsheets or tabs devoted to the target type (i.e., keywords, categories, and products).

When you launch the next campaign for the same book, use the HPKs to focus your ad while using the negative targeting to suppress your ad where it's known for poor conversions. Building a campaign based on previous data is what I like to refer to as a Tier 2 ad. The next iterations would be Tier 3, Tier 4, and so on.

However, I stress caution and recommend lowering your expectations when launching new campaigns. Despite the fact that you're using HPKs and negative targeting based on previous results and your own analysis, a new ad campaign is still "new."

Since you're starting a new ad, Amazon only has the product sales history to determine relevancy. The ad has no relevance, so what you might think is going to perform great may not deliver much at first. You'll have to tweak this ad just like you did the first version. While you might have had significant results for a set of targets, this ad may not convert as well for these targets.

Does that mean you should remove them? No, let it play out. If you find some HPKs aren't converting as well as you'd like, simply lower the bid or pause them altogether.

If you have the budget to handle multiple ads, I recommend trying it. Simply firing off one ad is only going to get you so much information. The more ads you have in play, the more opportunity you have to analyze and tweak future iterations. You'll find moderate success on a Tier 1 ad, but the real magic happens when you're about three or four tiers deep into the process.

Does this spread your marketing budget thin? Possibly, but if you bid low and scale slow, you shouldn't blow through your ad budget. In fact, you'll find that unlike Facebook or Google ads, Amazon won't spend your daily limit. It's kind of crazy, but Amazon simply doesn't want your money if the ad doesn't serve the customer best. That's not to say your ad or your book is rubbish, it's just a sign that:

- Your CPC is too low to serve
- Your ad isn't relevant to the targeting
- Your ad hasn't had time to age

Will Amazon blow through your budget if you bid low on everything? It's highly unlikely, but it is possible. I never had an issue with bidding low and scaling slow. Heck, I had ads set with a daily budget of $100 with low CPCs (around $0.10 to $0.15) and the ad only spent $12 for the month with a few conversions. While I can speculate on what Amazon does, my opinions won't necessarily reflect what Amazon may actually do.

I'm sure in due time Amazon Advertising will catch up with their contemporaries (i.e., Facebook ads, Google ads) and they'll blow through your budget whether you bid low or high. For now, enjoy the golden era of Amazon Advertising. It may not last. Authors with limited budgets will have few alternatives to promote their books on Amazon.

While I've given you enough information to be dangerous, you may have questions. Let's take a deeper look at some common issues and how to solve them.

TROUBLESHOOTING A PROBLEMATIC AD

In a perfect world, you could simply read this book, buy a course, or have a friend walk you through Amazon Advertising. Turn on those ads, and boom! You're an overnight success. The reality is more people fail at using Amazon Advertising than succeed.

Why is that?

Many advertisers don't have the patience or the budget to advertise long-term on Amazon. You can't expect to run a few ads and become a success. The reality is you're going to have to learn the process through doing it. With so many variables at play, I even debated over whether to write a book about Amazon ads because of the minefield of issues all advertisers have.

Rather than write an FAQ section, I figured we'd cover some miscellaneous items in separate sections. Do yourself a favor and don't simply cherry-pick. A lot of details shared in this book work well together and are less effective apart. I'm showing you a much larger picture than simply one item at a time.

For all my best efforts, I won't cover some topics. Often, Amazon Advertising will change their features or add new options. Though I'd love to pump out a new edition every time they make a change, that's not very realistic. With that said, know that I've done my best to provide you the most up-to-date info as of the time of this writing. Should any major changes come about after publishing this book, I'll most likely update the book and add more to this section. Let's dig into troubleshooting your problematic ads.

BIDDING STRATEGIES FOR ADS

When starting Amazon ads, always keep your daily budget and your CPC low. It's better to start low and slow than to rip into a deep budget with high CPCs. I worked with a new author once who started with CPCs at or over $1 and a daily budget of $1,000. Shockingly, he'd never used the ads platform before and was merely throwing money at the problem. Sure, the author got about 12 sales within a few days, but he also received a $3,000 bill for running only a couple of ads on a few books.

The best way to get into Amazon Advertising is to run an ad at $1 to $10 per day and keep your CPCs obnoxiously low around $0.10 to $0.15. Will you have to increase the bids? Absolutely! As mentioned previously, if you see that some targets get no impressions, then Amazon is giving you a clear sign your bids are way too low to get placement. Give a target at least 72 hours to perform before increasing the bid by a few cents. If you're feeling rather bold, you can always use the suggested bids as a guidepost.

For instance, when I see an underperforming target, I'll consider the range for suggested bid. Let's say the suggested bid is between $0.75 to $1.25. Maybe my current bid is $0.15. I know that $0.75 is probably my limit and $1.25 is way past my comfort zone. I still want to try placement for the target, so I'll hit the lower end of the suggested bidding range around $0.75, hoping to get traction. Should the CPC be out of reach, I'll keep the bid low and let it ride a few more days.

I've heard Amazon recommend this strategy: if a target isn't converting as well as you'd like but is still relevant to the product, *decrease* the bid. They don't address if keeping a target at a lower bid will decrease the relevancy of the ad. Personally, when I find a target isn't performing well, I pause it so the ad can devote more budget to targets that are cheaper or converting better.

Running Amazon ads is much like growing multiple plants in one pot. With limited nutrients in the soil, each plant only gets so much nutrition. When you remove one plant from the pot, the other plants have more nutrients than before. The same works for your individual ad. When you have tons of targeting in one ad, prune those targets when they aren't serving the campaign well.

The next bidding strategy relies on how much traction you have with the advertised book (aka sales velocity). If you're getting dozens of sales per day without ads before you start using ads, then you might find the bidding a bit confusing. While the suggested bids might be ridiculously high, you don't have to go with that. In fact, if you're dominating your niche, you can bid absurdly low and actually win.

Why is that?

Relevancy! Once Amazon sees you're advertising a product that has consistent sales performance month after month, they're happy to give you the nod. The more relevant your product is to the algorithm, the easier ads can be.

Another bidding strategy to consider is with Tier 2 ads or greater. Once you identify HPKs and start a new ad with them, what bid do you place on the targets? The straightforward answer is to stick with the average CPC for the HPK of the previous ad campaign. You can also use the suggested bid, but again, it might not be workable based on your previous results. This means if you converted well on a target at $0.98 and the suggested bid is $2.25, then I'd lean in favor of the cheaper option. You can always increase the bid if you're not getting impressions in the first few days.

Using that same bidding strategy, you can try using the bid at a slight increase, so long as it doesn't eat into your profits. Bidding a wee bit higher might increase the likelihood of preferential placement of your ad.

Bidding strategies are unending, and you might find your own way with time and practice. No single bidding strategy fits all advertisers. Much like gambling at a casino, every gambler has their method for winning. The only way to know your preferred strategy is through trial and error. It's not sexy and doesn't make for a great headline, but it's true. Test a lot, fail a lot, analyze the results, and adjust your approach.

HELP! SOMEONE IS GETTING MY SALES

When a customer clicks on your ad, they're directed to your book's product page. From there, customers have the choice of all your options, including ebooks, print books, audiobooks, and third-party sellers. It's the latter option that leaves authors confused and worried if they're getting duped. On most occasions, a third-party seller is legit. They have a used copy of your book and are allowed

TROUBLESHOOTING A PROBLEMATIC AD

to sell it on Amazon. The nice part is you know the third party had or a previous reader had to buy a copy of your book in order for it be available used.

In the event a customer buys the third-party option, then you will not get credit for the sale. Yes, you sent people to your page with an ad, and you should get credit for all sales. Sadly, that's not always the case.

To further complicate the issue, Amazon has a feature called the **Buy Box** where a specific vendor or seller gets prime placement on the product page. When a customer adds the item to their cart, Amazon will default to the seller with the **Buy Box**.

If you ever feel like a seller is using unscrupulous tactics, report it to Amazon or ask for clarification from the seller. Worst-case scenario is you buy the book to make sure it isn't a pirated version. Should you find that it is, report the seller to Amazon immediately. You'll know if the publication is fake based on the content. Often, book pirates don't pay attention to the fine details like you, so you can discover those things, highlight them, and share it with Amazon.

Will you get your ad spend back? No, because the purpose of ads is to drive traffic to the page and not to guide customers to buy specific products from specific sellers.

Authors publishing through KDP should, in theory, always get the Buy Box. We have no control over that since the Amazon algorithm determines what's most likely to convert a sale. Again, as I've said many times, Amazon wants to please the customer, so if that means placing a different seller in the top position, they will.

CROSSCHECKING ADS

Never rely solely on the Amazon Advertising dashboard to give you the clearest picture. Between the 72-hour delay and the 14-day cookie tracking, your ads dashboard will not be entirely accurate. That's why you should use the Amazon Ads dashboard along with another tracking tool to analyze your results.

Not everyone is going to buy your book after seeing your ad once. Sometimes, they'll come back to buy your book at a later date even after the tracking period for the ad. Running effective ads doesn't always mean you're going to have direct results. The point of advertising is to be more visible online and to convert interest to sales. With diligent efforts and consistency running ads, you'll see a ripple effect in your entire catalog of books.

Enter Book Report.

As covered previously, Book Report is a trusted tool among many industry experts and established KDP authors, so you're in good hands. Why would you choose *Book Report* over the KDP dashboard to track sales? KDP doesn't have the best user interface in the Reports tab. Recently, KDP rolled out an updated **Reports** interface, but they're still working on some bugs. Report any issues you run into because they won't know there is a problem unless you tell them.

Rather than relying on a questionable sales dashboard, install the browser extension. Those of you making above $1,000 per month won't miss the money invested in the app, since it'll save you a lot of time.

What do you do with *Book Report* then? Open your Amazon Ads dashboard and *Book Report* in two separate tabs in your browser.

Now, isolate the dates your ad serves on in both tabs. *Book Report* will show you actual sales while Amazon Ads will show you less. Why? Well, it's just so stinking delayed.

In your Amazon Advertising dashboard, you'll see gross sales but not net profits. With *Book Report*, net profits and each profit will be broken down by sales across ebooks, print books, and KENP reads.

Should you find *Book Report* not to be your thing, or if you don't want to pay for it, you can find what is working by having your KDP and Amazon Ads dashboards open. I expect some day, KDP will refine the **Reports** feature. Until then, we just have to hope for the best with the information we have between the two accounts.

CONCLUSION

Reflecting on my brief tenure in multi-level marketing, I realize it wasn't a total waste. Did I lose money? Yep! Would I do it again? Absolutely not. The valuable lesson I learned from running an MLM business was that spending money to make money is a risky strategy. In fact, the odds are more likely in your favor at a casino. Heck, even then, you might get a complimentary cocktail without having to sell it to another sucker.

Much like my experience in MLM, I discovered running Amazon Ads can be just as risky, especially if you don't know what you're doing. Fortunately for you, I'm not trying to indoctrinate you into the Amazon Advertising business model. Whether you use this guide to grow your self-publishing business is going to be up to you. Sure, results may vary, but I'm confident if you have the budget, the patience, and the time to work in pay-per-click ads, then you might just move the needle in your author business today.

The thing you're going to need in order to be successful in Amazon Advertising is a budget, time, patience, and a willingness to learn as you go. While you could read this book repeatedly, it ultimately won't do anything for you unless you take action. Only you can pull the trigger. Prepare to suffer some setbacks and even question your sanity for investing in Amazon Ads. As soon as you get it, you'll *really* get it. You'll have a light bulb moment that'll change how you see and use Amazon Ads. Once you do, you'll thank yourself for never giving up and always pushing forward despite the odds.

While I don't recommend going into multi-level marketing, I do suggest authors consider using Amazon ads to sell more books. After all, you're putting yourself at a greater advantage than authors who don't use this avenue. You'll sell more books, build more relevancy in the Amazon algorithm, and uncover a new treasure trove of eager readers who might've never found you without the power of Amazon Advertising. Will you spend money? Yes! Will all that money garner positive results? No, at least not at first.

Take your time with Amazon Advertising. Be okay with taking a few missteps and making mistakes. The worst problem that can come of those issues is an unwillingness to figure out where you went wrong. Also, there's absolutely nothing wrong with reaching out to a peer in this industry who's currently using Amazon Ads. Network and mastermind with other authors who use pay-per-click ads so you have a sounding board of like-minded professionals with your best interests at heart.

I highly recommend joining my Discord community to connect with other authors like you at DaleLinks.com/Discord. Also, between two YouTube channels and over 1,500 videos to date, you'll find answers to most every question about self-publishing. Visit my main channel at YouTube.com/@DaleLRoberts and my podcast channel at YouTube.com/@SelfPubWithDale.

Finally, while I admit Amazon Advertising isn't for everyone, it can be for most anyone willing to take a gamble on themselves. After all, it's not the ads that bring in the results, it's you. You get to determine where your ads go and who gets to see your ad. You get to decide how much money to invest and when to pull the plug. If it was as simple as running an automated targeting campaign, then everyone would do it. If you have enough faith in yourself, the right budget, and a willingness to learn, then Amazon Advertising is for you.

Good luck!

A SMALL ASK...

Now that you've finished reading this book, what did you think of what you read? Were there any insights you found helpful? What do you think was missing from this book? While you're thinking back on what you read, it'd mean the world to me if you left an honest review from where you purchased or downloaded this book.

Reviews play an integral part in building relevancy for all products across numerous online retail platforms. Whether you found the information helpful or lacking in some areas, your candid review will help other customers make an informed purchase.

Also, based on your review, I'll adjust this publication and future editions. That way, you and other indie authors can learn and grow.

Leave a review at DaleLinks.com/ReviewAdsBook.

GET MORE BOOK SALES TODAY!

You wrote the book.

And now it's published.

But you're not getting any sales! What gives?!

Most people would have you believe self-publishing on Amazon is easy. Yet why aren't you seeing the results they claim you should?

A lack of book sales comes down to three culprits:

- Keywords
- Marketing and promotion
- Book reviews

It's time you put all your self-publishing woes to bed and finally increase your book sales for good.

Enter *The Amazon Self-Publisher*.

You'll learn:

- The secrets to keyword research and selection
- Cheap yet effective book promotions
- How to get book reviews the legit way

- Where Amazon Advertising will serve your book best

And hundreds of powerful insights!

You'll love learning all about Amazon self-publishing, because once you discover proven strategies in self-publishing, your life will change for the better.

Order this three-part series in one book now when you visit:

DaleLinks.com/SelfPubBook

ABOUT THE AUTHOR

Dale L. Roberts is a prolific author and video content creator. Dale's inherent passion for life fuels his self-publishing advocacy both in print and online. After publishing over 50 titles and becoming an award-winning and international bestselling author on Amazon, Dale started his YouTube channel, *Self-Publishing with Dale*. Since publishing his first book in 2014, Dale has cemented his position as the go-to authority in the indie author community.

Dale currently lives with his wife Kelli and two rescue cats in Columbus, Ohio.

Relevant links:

- My Books—DaleLinks.com/Bookshelf
- Website—SelfPublishingWithDale.com
- YouTube—DaleLinks.com/YouTube
- Podcast—DaleLinks.com/YouTubePodcast
- Discord—DaleLinks.com/Discord

SPECIAL THANKS

While in my previous books, I thanked everyone under the sun, I narrowed it down to just a few. Without them, I wouldn't be able to accomplish as much as I have.

Big thank you to my wife, Kelli, because without her, I'd most likely be still working a day job and not really even feeling as ambitious as I am now. I owe a lot to this woman, and I kindly ask you to search up her YouTube channel, subscribe, and tell her I sent you.

My immense gratitude and love go to Jeanne De Vita. Your calm, reassuring voice has always guided me to better writing and I'm forever grateful for all the knowledge and insights you've poured into my business. You are priceless!

Also, thank you, reader. With thousands of experts and insiders, you actively chose to invest your time and money into my book. Your investment and trust are nothing I take lightly, so that's why I pour my heart and soul into every manuscript.

RESOURCES

- Amazon Advertising Certification Courses – Advertising.Amazon.com
- Amazon Author Central – Author.Amazon.com
- Book Report – GetBookReport.com/Install
- Publisher Rocket – DaleLinks.com/Rocket
- *Amazon Ads Unleashed* by Robert Ryan – DaleLinks.com/RyanBook
- *Mastering Amazon Ads* by Brian Meeks – DaleLinks.com/MeeksBook1
- *Mastering Amazon Descriptions* by Brian Meeks – DaleLinks.com/MeeksBook
- *How to Write a Sizzling Synopsis* by Bryan Cohen – DaleLinks.com/Sizzling
- *Amazon Ads for Authors* by Ricardo Fayet – DaleLinks.com/Ricardo
- *Amazon Ads for Indie Authors* by Janet Margot – DaleLinks.com/Janet

REFERENCES

[i] Amazon.com LLC. (No date). Amazon Advertising Certification Course. https://learningconsole.amazonadvertising.com/uploads/resource_courses/targets/25787/original/index.html?_courseId=339#/page/5df02994009a452ced83c872

[ii] Amazon.com, LLC. (No date). Amazon Advertising Course. https://learningconsole.amazonadvertising.com/uploads/resource_courses/targets/25747/original/index.html?_courseId=335#/page/5df7979e82a0716237f06c18

[iii] Amazon.com, LLC. (No date). CPC (Cost per Click) explained. https://advertising.amazon.com/library/guides/cost-per-click

[iv] Amazon.com, LLC. (No Date). Amazon Advertising Certification Course. https://learningconsole.amazonadvertising.com/uploads/resource_courses/targets/25775/original/index.html?_courseId=337#/page/5de6ae270707a72fcc24bbb8

[v] Amazon.com, LLC. (No Date). Amazon Advertising Certification Course. https://learningconsole.amazonadvertising.com/uploads/resource_courses/targets/25747/original/index.html?_courseId=335#/page/5df7979e82a0716237f06c18

[vi]Amazon.com, LLC. (No date). Advertising billing. https://advertising.amazon.com/help?entityId=ENTITY2358XJVOPHN6&ref=AA_unav_support_center#GUJY2CG5DTCPDCVQ.

[vii]Amazon.com, LLC. (No date). Amazon Advertising Certification Course. https://learningconsole.amazonadvertising.com/uploads/resource_courses/targets/25775/original/index.html?_courseId=337#/page/5de6ae270707a72fcc24bc06.

[viii]Amazon.com, LLC. (No date). Understanding advertising charges. https://advertising.amazon.com/help?entityId=ENTITY2358XJVOPHN6#GY3YNTWRZYVPLADL.

[ix]Chesson, D. (17 June 2022). Kindle Keyword Ranking Percentages: #1 vs. #2. https://kindlepreneur.com/kindle-keyword-ranking-percentages-1-vs-2/

[x]Amazon Ads. (no date). Bidding on keywords (module). https://learningconsole.amazonadvertising.com/uploads/resource_courses/targets/61311/original/index.html?_courseId=4798#/page/63d15f6321a5970b817b4caa

[xi]Amazon Ads. (no date). Bidding on keywords (module). https://learningconsole.amazonadvertising.com/uploads/resource_courses/targets/61311/original/index.html?_courseId=4798#/page/63d15f6321a5970b817b4caa

www.ingramcontent.com/pod-product-compliance
Lightning Source LLC
Chambersburg PA
CBHW060032040426
42333CB00042B/2311